Basic German Dictionary-Grammar

A Dictionary containing the 2500 most
commonly used words, with the essentials
of German grammar

John Murray
50 Albemarle Street
London, England

EMC Corporation
180 East Sixth Street
St Paul, Minnesota, USA

Printed in Great Britain by
Redwood Burn Limited, Trowbridge & Esher

John Murray   EMC Corporation
ISBN 0 7195 3076 8   ISBN 0 88436 183 7

Preface

This book is designed as a basic tool for anyone learning German—regardless of what method is being used to approach the language or of the individual learner's ability. Both the Dictionary and the Grammar sections are carefully organised for ease of reference and their combination provides a wide range of vocabulary and grammatical information not normally available in single volume form.

The Dictionary section contains the 2500 German words which form perhaps 90% of current printed matter and speech. The Grammer section covers the essentials without going into fine—and confusing—detail and provides all that is needed for a working knowledge of the language.

In compiling the Dictionary the following sources, in particular, have been used: Oehler's *Grundwortschatz Deutsch* and Pfeffer's *Grunddeutsch*. The publishers are also grateful for work done by Henning Madsen and the editorial team of Grafisk Forlag, Copenhagen.

The letters A, B or C by entries in the Dictionary indicate that a word falls within the confines of the word lists used as the basis for the first three grades of the series of German *Easy Readers* published by EMC Corporation and John Murray. The Dictionary as a whole corresponds to the D series of readers.

Contents

Dictionary

Abbreviations

adj.	adjective	*n*	neuter
adv.	adverb	*past part.*	past participle
art.	article	*pl.*	plural
card.	cardinal number	*prep.*	preposition
comp.	comparative	*pres. part.*	present participle
conj.	conjunction	*pron.*	pronoun
dat.	dative	*subst.*	noun
f	feminine	*sup.*	superlative
interj.	interjection	*w.v.*	weak verb
m	masculine		

Nouns

1. The genitive singular ending of masculine and neuter nouns is given.
2. For all nouns which have plurals the plural ending is given.

Verbs

1. Weak verbs are marked *w.v.*
2. For strong and mixed verbs the vowel changes are given, i.e. 2nd and 3rd person singular Present tense
   Imperfect
   Past Participle
   Example: abnehmen i/a/o
   Er nimmt ab
   Ich nahm ab
   Wir haben abgenommen
3. A few verbs have the vowel changes and the endings -te(-, n, t,) in the Imperfect and -t in the Past Participle. These endings are not given in the text.
   Example: bringen i/a/a
   Er bringt
   Ich brachte
   Wir haben gebracht

A

ab A *(adv.+prep.)* off; down; away; from; *ab heute* from to-day; *ab und zu* now and again

Abend B -s, -e *m* evening, night; *am Abend* in the evning; *heute abend* tonight, this evening

Abendessen D -s, - *n* dinner, supper

abends C *(adv.)* in the evening; at night

aber A *(conj.)* but, however

abfahren B ä/u/a leave, start

Abfahrt D -en *f* departure, start

abhängen [von] D ä/i/a depend [on]; *das hängt von dir ab* that depends on you

abholen B *(w.v.)* fetch, meet, go to meet, call for

abladen C ä/u/a unload, unpack, dump

abmachen D *(w.v.)* arrange, settle; *abgemacht!* it's a bargain!

abnehmen C i/a/o take off, remove; lose weight

abreißen C ei/i/i tear off/away, pull down

Abschied C -s, -e *m* departure, fare-well; *Abschied nehmen* take leave of, bid farewell

abschließen C ie/o/o lock (up); close

Absicht C -en *f* intention, purpose; *mit Absicht* on purpose

Abteilung D -en *f* division; group, class; department

abwärts D *(adv.)* down, downwards

ach! C *(interj.)* oh!, alas!, you don't say!; *ach so!* oh, I see!

achten auf C *(w.v.)* respect; take care of, pay attention to

achtgeben [auf] C i/a/e look [out]; take care [of]

Achtung A *f* respect, regard; *Achtung!* look out!, beware!

Adresse C -n *f* address

ähnlich A *(adj.)* (a)like, similar to; *er sieht seinem Vater ähnlich* he looks like his father; *das sieht ihm ähnlich* that is just like him

alle A *(adj.)* all; everybody; *alle beide* both of them; *alle acht Tage* once a week

allein A *(adj. + conj.)* alone, single

aller- C *(with sup.)* very; of all; by far [in compounds with adjectives in the superlative]

allerdings A *(adv.)* certainly, indeed

alles A *(pron.)* all, everything; *alles in allem* all in all

allgemein A *(adj.)* general, usual; universal; *im allgemeinen* in general, generally

als A *(conj.)* when; than; as; *als ob* as if; *sobald als* as soon as

also A *(adv.)* so, thus. *(conj.)* consequently

alt A *(adj.)* old; aged; ancient; used; *er ist 5 Jahre alt* he is 5 years old; *alte Geschichte* ancient history; *alte Bücher* second-hand books

Alter C -s, - *n* age; old age

am = **an dem**

Amt B -es, ⁼er *n* office; department; charge; post; position

an A *(prep.)* at, against, by, in, on, to; *an sich* in itself; *es ist nicht an dem* it is not so; *von nun an* henceforth

anbieten C ie/o/o offer; present

Anblick B -s *m* sight; aspect, view; *beim ersten Anblick* at first sight

ander A *(adj.)* other, different; *ein anderer* another; *unter anderem* among other things; *nichts anders* nothing else

ändern B *(w.v.)* alter, change, modify; *es ist nicht zu ändern* it cannot be helped

anders A *(adv.)* differently, otherwise; *ich kann nicht anders* I cannot help; *jemand anders* somebody else

anderswo [hin] C *(adv.)* elsewhere

anerkennen D e/a/a acknowledge, recognize; admit

Anfang A -s, ⁼e *m* beginning, start; *am Anfang* at/in the beginning; *von Anfang bis Ende* from start to finish

anfangen A ä/i/a begin, set about, start; *von vorn anfangen* to begin again

anfangs B *(adv.)* at first, at/in the beginning

Angebot D -s, -e *n* offer

Angelegenheit C -en *f* affair; concern, matter, business

angenehm B *(adj.)* pleasant, agreeable; *sehr angenehm* glad to meet you

angreifen C ei/i/i attack; take hold of

Angriff C -s, -e *m* attack; assault; *in Angriff nehmen* set about, begin with

Angst C ⁔e *f* anxiety, fear; *Angst haben* be afraid; *mir ist Angst* I'm afraid

ängstlich B *(adj.)* anxious, fearful; careful

anhalten B ä/ie/a arrest, stop

anklagen [**wegen** *or genitive*] B *(w.v.)* accuse [of]; charge [with]

ankommen B o/a/o 1. arrive, come, get to, reach; *der Zug kommt um 4 Uhr an* the train arrives at 4 o'clock. 2. *es kommt auf dich an* it depends on you

anmachen B *(w.v.)* put on, switch on

annehmen A i/a/o 1. accept; *er hat den Vorschlag angenommen* he has accepted the proposal. 2. suppose; *nehmen wir an* suppose

Anruf C -s, -e *m* call

anrufen B u/ie/u hail; call (up); ring up; *ich rufe dich heute abend an* I'll call you tonight

ansehen A ie/a/e 1. look at; view. 2. consider, look upon

Ansicht B -en *f* sight; view, opinion; *meiner Ansicht nach* in my opinion

anständig B *(adj.)* decent, proper, honest

Antwort A -en *f* answer, reply; *in Antwort auf* in reply to

antworten A *(w.v.)* answer, reply; give an answer

anwenden C e/a/a apply, employ, use

Anwendung D -en *f* application, use

Anzeige C -n *f* advertisement; notice; information

anziehen B ie/o/o 1. dress, put on. 2. attract, draw; *anziehend* attractive

Anzug B -s, ⁔e *m* suit; *den Anzug anziehen* put on one's suit

anzünden D *(w.v)* light, kindle; *ein Streichholz anzünden* light a match

Apfel B -s, ⸚ *m* apple

Apfelsine C -n *f* orange

Apotheke C -n *f* chemist's shop; pharmacy

Apparat B -s, -e *m* apparatus; instrument; *Radioapparat* wireless set; *am Apparat!* speaking! (on the phone)

Arbeit A -en *f* work; labour; *Arbeit suchen* look for a job; *arbeitslos* out of work, unemployed

arbeiten A *(w.v.)* work; *schwer arbeiten* work hard

Arbeiter A -s, - *m* worker, workman

Arm A -s, -e *m* arm

arm A *(adj.)* poor

Art A -en *f* kind, sort; manner, fashion, way; *auf diese Art und Weise* in this way; *auf deutsche Art* in the German way

Artikel D -s, - *m* article

Arzt B -es, ⸚e *m* physician, doctor

Ast C -es, ⸚e *m* branch

Atem C -s *m* breath; breathing; *Atem holen* catch one's breath; *den Atem anhalten* hold one's breath

auch A *(adv.)* also, too; *auch nicht* nor, neither; *wer auch* whoever; *auch schon* already

auf A *(prep.)* on, upon; in, into; of; at; by; for; to

Aufenthalt C -s, -e *m* stop, stay

auffallen D ä/ie/a strike; surprise; astonish; *auffallend* striking, remarkable

Aufgabe A -n *f* task, duty; homework, lesson

aufgehen D e/i/a rise; open

aufhängen D ä/i/a hang up

aufheben B e/o/o 1. pick up. 2. keep, put away. 3. dissolve, break up/off

aufhören A *(w.v.)* stop, break off; *hör auf damit!* stop it!

aufmachen A *(w.v.)* open; *den Mund aufmachen* speak up

aufmerksam B *(adj.)* attentive, polite

Aufmerksamkeit B -en *f* attention; politeness; *Aufmerksamkeit erweisen* [*auf*] pay attention [to]

Aufnahme C -n *f* taking/shooting of pictures; recording; photo; admission; *Aufnahmen machen* take photographs/pictures, make recordings

aufnehmen B i/a/o receive, take in, admit; photograph; *er hat es übel aufgenommen* he has resented it

aufpassen A *(w.v.)* look out for, watch; take care of; pay attention to; mind; *aufgepaßt!* look out!

aufstehen A e/a/a get up, rise

aufstellen C *(w.v.)* set up; install; *eine Liste aufstellen* make out a list

Auftrag D -s,ṣe *m* order; command; commission; charge; *im Auftrage von* by order of

aufwärts D *(adv.)* up; upward(s)

Auge A -s, -n *n* eye; *unter vier Augen* in private, face to face; *in die Augen fallen* strike/catch the eye; *ins Auge sehen* face; *im Auge behalten* keep in sight/mind

Augenblick B -s, -e *m* moment; instant; *im Augenblick* for the moment

aus A *(prep.)* from; of; through; for; in; by; on; *von mir aus* for my part; *von Grund aus* thoroughly

aus D *(adv.)* over; out; *es ist aus damit* that's the end of it

Ausbildung C -en *f* education; training; development

Ausdruck C -s,ṣe *m* expression; phrase; term; *zum Ausdruck bringen* express

Ausfahrt C -en *f* 1. exit; way out. 2. ride; excursion

ausführen D *(w.v.)* 1. carry out; perform. 2. export

Ausgang B -s,ṣe *m* 1. exit; way out. 2. going out. 3. day-off; *Unglücksfall mit tödlichem Ausgang* fatal accident

ausgeben C i/a/e spend; give out

ausgeschlossen [!] D *(adj + interj.)* impossible!; out of the question

aushalten C ä/ie/a suffer; stand; bear; endure

Auskunft Dṣe *f* information

Ausland D -s *n* foreign country; *im/ins Ausland* abroad; *ausländisch* foreign

auslöschen B *(w.v.)* quench, extinguish; put out; switch off

ausmachen B *(w.v.)* 1. put out; switch off. 2. make up; amount to; *das macht nichts aus!* never mind!

Ausnahme D -n *f* exception; *mit Ausnahme* excepting

ausrufen C **u/ie/u** cry out; exclaim

ausruhen A *(w.v.)* rest; take a rest

ausschalten C *(w.v.)* turn out; switch off

aussehen A **ie/a/e** appear; look; *aussehen wie* look like; *wie sieht es aus?* how is it?

außen C *(adv.)* out; out of doors; [on the] outside; *von außen* from outside

außer B *(prep.)* out of; outside; beyond; apart from; *außer Gefahr* out of danger; *außer Betrieb* out of order

außerdem A *(adv.)* besides; what is more

außerhalb C *(prep.)* beyond; without; outside; *von außerhalb* from abroad

äußere D *(adj.)* exterior; outward

außergewöhnlich B *(adj.)* extraordinary; unusual

Aussicht B -en *f* view; look out; chance; *in Aussicht stellen* promise

aussprechen C **i/a/o** pronounce

aussteigen C **ei/ie/ie** get off/out; step off/out

Ausstellung D -en *f* exhibition; show; fair

Ausweis D -es, -e *m* identity card; pass

auswendig C *(adj.)* outside; by heart; *auswendig können* know by heart

auswischen D *(w.v.)* wipe out

ausziehen B **ie/o/o** take off; *sich ausziehen* undress, strip

Auto A -s, -s *n* car, motor-car; *Auto fahren* drive a car

B

backen C **ä/uk/a** bake (past tense also: *backte*)

Bad B -es, ̈er *n* bath; bathe; swimming pool

baden A *(w.v.)* bath, bathe; take/have a bath

Bahn B -en *f* railway; line; *mit der Bahn fahren* go by train

bald A *(adv.)* soon; early; almost; *möglichst bald* as soon as possible; *ich wäre bald gefallen* I nearly fell

Ball A -s, ⸚e *m* ball

Band C -es, ⸚er *n* ribbon; tape; bandage

Band D -es, ⸚e *m* volume

Bank A ⸚e *f* bench; seat

Bank A -en *f* bank; banking house

basteln D *(w.v.)* tinker; potter; make models; do handicraft; "do it yourself"

Bau B -s, -ten *m* building; construction

Bau B -s, -e *m* burrow; den; *der Bau des Fuchses* the fox's earth

Bauch C -es, ⸚e *m* belly; stomach; abdomen

Bauer A -s, -n *m* farmer; peasant

Baum A -es, ⸚e *m* tree

Beamte[r] C -n, -n *m* civil servant; official

Bedarf D -s *m* need; requirement; want; demand; *nach Bedarf* when required

bedauern D *(w.v.)* regret; feel sorry

bedecken C *(w.v.)* cover (with); screen; protect

bedeuten B *(w.v.)* mean; stand for; *es hat nichts zu bedeuten* it is of no consequence

Bedeutung B -en *f* meaning; importance

bedienen C *(w.v.)* serve; attend, wait on

Bedingung C -en *f* condition, term; *unter der Bedingung, daß* provided that

beenden A *(w.v.)* end; finish; put an end to

Befehl C -s, -e *m* order; command; *auf Befehl* by order

befehlen C ie/a/o order; command; tell; *befehlen über* dispose of

begegnen D *(w.v.)* meet; happen, occur

Beginn B -s *m* beginning; start

beginnen B i/a/o begin; start; commence

begleiten B *(w.v.)* accompany; attend; go with; *nach Hause begleiten* see someone home

Begriff D **-s, -e** *m* idea; understanding; *im Begriff(e) sein* be about to

behalten A **ä/ie/a** 1. keep. 2. remember

behandeln C *(w.v.)* treat; handle; *schlecht behandeln* ill-treat

behaupten B *(w.v.)* assert; state; say; *es wird behauptet* it is claimed/asserted

Behörde D **-n** *f* authority; authorities

bei A *(prep.)* at; by; near; in; with; on; among; *bei weitem* by far; *bei deiner Ankunft* on your arrival

beide A *(adj.)* both; *einer von beiden* one of the two; *zu beiden Seiten* on either side

beim = **bei dem**

Bein A **-es, -e** *n* leg; bone; *früh auf den Beinen sein* be up early

beinahe A *(adv.)* almost; nearly

Beispiel B **-s, -e** *n* example; instance; *zum Beispiel (z.B.)* for example/instance (e.g.)

beißen B **ei/i/i** bite; *ins Gras beißen* bite the dust

bekannt A *(adj.)* known; well-known; *es ist mir bekannt* I know that

Bekannte[r] C **-n, -n** *m (adj. used as noun)* acquaintance; *ein Bekannter von mir* a friend of mine

Bekanntmachung D **-en** *f* notice; proclamation; announcement

bekommen A **o/a/o** get; receive; obtain; *was bekommen Sie?* what do I owe you?

beladen D **ä/u/a** load; *beladen mit* laden with

beliebt D *(adj.)* favourite; beloved; popular

belohnen D *(w.v.)* reward

bemerken A *(w.v.)* realize; observe; remark; *bemerkenswert* remarkable

sich bemühen D *(w.v.)* try; take trouble; *darf ich Sie bemühen?* may I trouble you?

sich benehmen D **i/a/o** behave

benutzen A *(w.v.)* use; employ

beobachten A *(w.v.)* watch; observe

bequem A *(adj.)* suitable; convenient; comfortable; easy; at ease

bereit B *(adj.)* ready; *sich bereit halten* keep oneself ready

bereits B *(adv.)* already

Berg A -es, -e *m* mountain; hill; *über Berg und Tal* o'er hill and dale

Bericht B -s, -e *m* report; account

berichten B *(w.v.)* report; give an account; tell

Beruf B -es, -e *m* job, occupation; trade; profession; *von Beruf* by profession

berühmt C *(adj.)* noted; famous

berühren B *(w.v.)* touch; handle

beschäftigen B *(w.v.)* employ; occupy; give work to

beschließen D ie/o/o determine; make up one's mind

Beschluß D -sses, ⁻sse *m* decision; resolution; *zum Beschluß* in conclusion

Besen C -s, - *m* broom

besetzen D *(w.v.)* occupy; fill a vacancy

Besitz C -es *m* possession; property; (real) estate; *in Besitz nehmen* take possession

besitzen B i/a/e possess; own; have

besonder B *(adj.)* special; particular

besonders B *(adv.)* especially; particularly; chiefly

besorgen D *(w.v.)* provide [for]; see to; get; *besorge mir* get me

besser A *(adj. comp.)* better; *um so besser* all the better; *er ist besser dran* he is better off; *am besten* best

best C *(adj. sup.)* best; superior; *zu Ihrem besten* for your sake

bestehen [aus] B e/a/a consist [of]; be composed [of]; *ein Examen bestehen* pass; *nicht bestehen* fail

bestellen B *(w.v.)* order; book; ask; *bestellt sein* have an appointment; *schöne Grüße bestellen* give kind regards

bestimmen D *(w.v.)* determine; ascertain; estimate

bestimmt B *(adj.)* 1. decided; appointed. 2. firm

bestrafen [für] C *(w.v.)* punish [for]

Besuch C -es, -e *m* visit; call; *Besuch haben* have visitors; *auf Besuch* on a visit

besuchen B *(w.v.)* visit, go/come to see; attend

betrachten C *(w.v.)* look at; regard; consider

Betrag D -s, ⸚e *m* amount, value; sum; *im Betrag von* amounting to

betreffen D i/a/o concern; pertain to; *was das betrifft* as to that

betreten C i/a/e enter; *Betreten verboten!* no entrance!, keep off the grass!

Betrieb C -s, -e *m* works, plant; (work)shop; business; traffic; *in vollem Betrieb* in full action

Bett A -es, -en *n* bed; *am Bett* at the bedside; *zu Bett bringen* put to bed;

beurteilen D *(w.v.)* judge; review

Bevölkerung C -en *f* population

bevor D *(conj.)* before

bewegen A *(w.v.)* move

Beweis C -es, -e *m* proof; evidence

bezahlen B *(w.v.)* pay; *bar bezahlen* pay cash

bezeichnen C *(w.v.)* mark; label; indicate; *bezeichnend* characteristic

Beziehung C -en *f* relation; respect; regard; *in Beziehung stehen* be in relation with

Bier B -es, -e *n* beer

bieten B ie/o/o offer; present; bid

Bild A -es, -er *n* picture; painting; photo; image

bilden B *(w.v.)* form, shape; educate

billig C *(adj.)* 1. cheap. 2. fair, just

bin → **sein**

binden B i/a/u bind, tie

Birne D -n *f* 1. pear. 2. bulb (electric light)

bis A *(prep.)* till; until; *2 bis 3 Tage* two to three days

ein bißchen B a little; a (little) bit; a while

bist → **sein**

bitte A please; don't mention it; *wie bitte?* I beg your pardon?

Bitte B -n *f* request

bitten A i/a/e request; ask; beg; *zu Gast bitten* invite

bitter C *(adj.)* bitter

Blatt B -es, ⸚er *n* leaf; sheet [of paper]

blau A *(adj.)* blue

bleiben A ei/ie/ie stay; remain; *zu Hause bleiben* stay at home; *es bleibt dabei!* let us leave it at that! agreed!

Bleistift B -s, -e *m* pencil

Blick A -s, -e *m* look; glance; view; *auf den ersten Blick* at first sight

blind C *(adj.)* blind

Blitz D -es, -e *m* lightning; flash; *es blitzt* it is lightning

bloß A *(adv. and adj.)* only; simply; *mit bloßem Kopfe* bare-headed

blühen B *(w.v.)* bloom; blossom

Blume A -n *f* flower; *laßt Blumen sprechen!* say it with flowers!

Bluse D -n *f* blouse; tunic

Blut B -es *n* blood; *im Blut liegen* run in the blood

Boden A -s, ⸚ *m* ground; soil; floor; bottom; *auf dem Boden* on the ground/floor

Bord D -s, -e *m* board; *an Bord gehen* go on board; *über Bord* overboard

böse A *(adj.)* angry; evil; *böse Zeiten* hard times

braten C ä/ie/a roast; fry

brauchen A *(w.v.)* need; require; want; *Zeit brauchen* take time

braun C *(adj.)* brown

brechen A i/a/o break

breit A *(adj.)* broad; wide

brennen B e/a/a burn; be on fire; *er brannte darauf anzufangen* he was anxious to get started

Brett B -es, -er *n* board; plank; shelf

Brief B -es, -e *m* letter; note; *einen Brief zu Post geben* post/mail a letter; *Briefe wechseln[mit]* correspond [with]

Brille C -n *f* glasses; spectacles

bringen A i/a/a bring; fetch; take

Brot A -es, -e *n* bread; loaf of bread; *belegtes Brot* sandwich

Brücke C -n *f* bridge

Bruder A -s, ≝ *m* brother; *gleiche Brüder gleiche Kappen* share and share alike; we're all in the same boat

Brust B ≝e *f* breast; chest

Buch A -es, ≝er *m* book

Buchstabe D -n(s), -n *m* letter; character; type

bügeln D *(w.v.)* iron; press; smooth

Bühne D -n *f* stage; scene; theatre

bunt B *(adj.)* colourful; coloured; multicoloured

Bürger C -s, - *m* citizen; townsman

Büro C -s, -s *n* office; place of business

Bürste B -n *f* brush

bürsten D *(w.v.)* brush

Bus B -ses, -se *m* bus; coach

Butter B *f* butter

C

Charakter D -s, -e *m* character; temper

Chef C -s, -s *m* chief; head; employer

D

da A *(adv.)* (over) there; then; present; *hie und da* here and there, now and then; *da haben Sie es!* there you are!

da B *(conj.)* as; because

dabei B *(adv.)* near (by); close by; there; present; *was ist dabei?* what does it matter?

Dach B -s, ≝er *n* roof

dachte → **denken**

dadurch B *(adv.)* through there; that way; in that way

dafür B *(adv.)* for it/that; instead (of); in return for; *was kann ich dafür?* how can I help it?; *er ist dafür* he is in favour

dagegen B *(adv.)* against it/that; on the other hand

daher C *(adv.)* from there; for that reason; *daher kommt es, daß* hence it follows that

dahin A *(adv.)* there; past; gone, lost; *bis dahin* until then

dahinter C *(adv.)* behind that; beyond

damals B *(adv.)* then; at that time

Dame B **-n** *f* lady

damit B *(conj.)* with it/that; *heraus damit!* out with it!

Dampf D **-es,** ≃**e** *m* steam

danach B *(adv.)* later on; after it/that; accordingly; *bald danach* soon after

daneben B *(adv.)* near it/that

Dank B **-es** *m* thanks *(pl.)*; *Dank sagen* thank; *Gott sei Dank!* thank God!; *danke gleichfalls* thank you, the same to you

danken A *(w.v.)* thank

dann A *(adv.)* then; at that time; *und was dann?* and then what?; *dann erst* only then

daran C *(adv.)* at it/that; *er ist dran* it is his turn; *sie glaubt daran* she believes in it

darauf B *(adv.)* on it/that; afterwards

daraus C *(adv.)* out of it/that; *daraus folgt daß* hence it follows that

darf → **dürfen**

darin C *(adv.)* in it/that/there; within; *was ist darin?* what is inside?

darlegen D *(w.v.)* show; explain; state

darstellen C *(w.v.)* produce; picture; represent

darüber B *(adv.)* over/about it/that

darum B *(adv.)* about it/that; that's why

darunter B *(adv.)* under; below, among it/that/them

das A *(art.)* the

das A *(pron.)* who, whom, which, that, those; *das bin ich* it is I; *das sind Neger* those are negroes

daß A *(conj.)* that; *so daß* so that; *bis daß* till

dasselbe B *(pron.)* the same

dauern C *(w.v.)* last; take; *lange dauern* take long; *dauernd* constant

Daumen D -s, - *m* thumb

davon B *(adv.)* of/from it/that; *das kommt davon* that's the result of it

dazu A *(adv.)* to/with it/that; *noch dazu* besides

Decke A -n *f* 1. cover; blanket. 2. ceiling

Deckel D -s, - *m* lid

decken D *(w.v.)* cover; *den Tisch decken* set the table

dein, -e A *(poss. adj.)* your

deine, -r, -s A *(poss. pron.)* yours

denken [an] A e/a/a think [of]; reflect; *ich denke schon* I think so; *denken Sie mal!* just imagine!

denn B *(conj.)* for

dennoch B *(adv.)* yet; still; though, however, all the same

der A *(art.)* the

der A *(pron.)* that, this; he, it; who; which; that

derselbe B *(pron.)* the same

deshalb B *(adv.)* therefore; that is why

desto D *(adv.)* the; *desto besser* so much the better

deswegen B *(adv.)* that's why

deutlich C *(adj.)* clear; distinct

deutsch A *(adj.)* German; *ins Deutsche übersetzen* translate into German

Deutsche(r) B -n, -n *m* German; *die Deutschen* the Germans

Deutschland B -s *n* Germany; *nach Deutschland* to Germany

dich A *(pers. pron.)* you; yourself

dicht B *(adj.)* tight; dense; solid; thick

Dichter D -s, - *m* poet

dick A *(adj.)* thick, fat

die A *(art.)* the

die A *(pron.)* that, this; she, it; who, which; that

Dieb D -es, -e *m* thief; *haltet den Dieb!* stop thief!

dienen D *(w.v.)* serve; *einem Zweck dienen* serve a purpose

Dienst C -es, -e *m* service; office; work; *im Dienst* on duty; *in Dienst nehmen* engage

dieser, diese, dieses A *(pron.)* this, this one; the latter

diesmal D *(adv.)* this time/once

Ding A -es, -e *n* thing

dir A *(pers.pron. dat.)* (to) you

direkt C *(adv. and adj.)* directly; straight

Direktor D -s, -en *m* manager, director; head-master; principal [of a school]

doch A *(conj.)* yet; though; still, after all; *hilf mir doch!* do help me!

Doktor B -s, -en *m* doctor; *den Doktor holen* send for the doctor

Donner D -s *m* thunder; *es donnert* it's thundering

doppelt A *(adj.)* double; twice

Dorf B -s, ̈er *n* village

dort A *(adv.)* (over)there

dorthin A *(adv.)* there; that way

Draht D -es, ̈e *m* wire

drängen B *(w.v.)* press; *die Zeit drängt* time presses

draußen C *(adv.)* outside; out of doors

drehen C *(w.v.)* turn; twist; roll

dringend C *(pres. part.)* urgent; pressing

drinnen C *(adv.)* in it/that/there; within

drohen D *(w.v.)* threaten

drüben D *(adv.)* over there; on the other side

Druck C -s, ̈e *m* pressure; print

drucken C *(w.v.)* print

drücken A *(w.v.)* press; squeeze

du A *(pers. pron.)* you; *auf du und du stehen* be on intimate terms

dumm A *(adj.)* stupid; silly; dull; simple; *er is nicht so dumm* he knows better

dunkel A *(adj.)* dark; gloomy; obscure; *es wird dunkel* it gets dark; *dunkelblau* dark-blue

dünn A *(adj.)* thin; slender; slim

durch A *(prep.)* by; through, across; during; by means of; *durch die Post* by post/mail; *durch und durch* thoroughly

durchaus C *(adv.)* completely; quite; absolutely; *durchaus nicht* not at all, by no means

durcheinander D *(adv.)* confusedly; in disorder; *ich bin ganz durcheinander* I'm all confused/mixed up

Durchfahrt D **-en** *f* passage; passing; *Durchfahrt verboten!* no thoroughfare

durchführen D *(w.v.)* carry out; bring about

durchqueren D *(w.v.)* cross; traverse

Durchschnitt D **-s, -e** *m* average; mean; *den Durchschnitt nehmen* strike an average; *durchschnittlich* on average erage

durchsehen D **ie/a/e** see through; review

dürfen A **a/u/u** may; be allowed/permitted; *darf ich fragen* may I ask; *ich darf nicht* I must not, I'm not allowed

Durst A **-es** *m* thirst; *Durst haben* be thirsty

duschen D *(w.v.)* take a shower

Dutzend D **-s, -e** *n* dozen; *dutzendweise* by the dozen

E

eben C *(adj.)* even; level; smooth

eben B *(adv.)* just; *ich habe eben gegessen* I have just eaten; *eben!* exactly!

ebenfalls C *(adv.)* likewise, equally; too

ebenso A *(adv.)* just so; as well; *ebenso gut wie* as well as

echt C *(adj.)* true; real; pure

Ecke C **-n** *f* corner; *um die Ecke* (a)round the corner; *in der Ecke* in the corner

egal D *(adj.)* equal; alike; *das ist mir ganz egal* it's all the same to me

ehe D *(conj.)* before; until

Ehe C -n *f* marriage

eher B *(adv.)* earlier; sooner; rather; *nicht eher bis* not until

Ehre D -n *f* honour; *ihm zu Ehren* in his honour

ehren D *(w.v.)* honour; respect

Ei B -s, -er *n* egg; *faules Ei* rotten egg; *weiches Ei* soft-boiled egg; *hartes Ei* hard-boiled egg

eigen B *(adj.)* own; particular; strange

Eigenschaft C -en *f* quality; property; *in seiner Eigenschaft als* in his capacity as/of

eigentlich C *(adj.)* real; true; actual; *im eigentlichen Sinn des Wortes* in the literal sense of the word

Eigentum D -s, ⁔er *n* property; possession

Eile C *f* haste; rush; speed; *ich habe Eile* I'm in a hurry; *in aller Eile* in great haste

eilen C *(w.v.)* hasten; hurry

Eimer C -s, - *m* pail; bucket

ein A *(art.)* a, an

ein und aus D on and off

einander C *(pron.)* each other; one another; *neben einander* side by side

Eindruck D -s, ⁔e *m* impression; sensation

eine -r, -s A *(card.)* one

einfach A *(adj.)* plain; simple; *einfache Fahrkarte* single ticket

Einfahrt D -en *f* entrance; way in; *keine Einfahrt!* No entrance!

Einfluß D -sses, ⁔sse *m* influence; *Einfluß haben* have influence

einführen D *(w.v.)* bring in; introduce; import

Eingang B -s, ⁔e *m* entrance; entry; *Eingang verboten!* No entrance!

einige A *(pron. pl.)* some

einkaufen A *(w.v.)* shop; go shopping; buy

einladen C ä/u/a 1. load. 2. invite; ask

einmal A *(adv.)* once; some time; *noch einmal* once more; *auf einmal* suddenly

einrichten B *(w.v.)* arrange; establish; *sich einrichten* establish oneself

einschalten B *(w.v.)* switch/turn on

einst D *(adv.)* once; one day

einsteigen D ei/ie/ie get in/on; *einsteigen!* take your seats, please!

einstellen C *(w.v.)* tune in; stop; regulate; set

eintreten B i/a/e enter; get in; join

Eintritt C -s *m* entrance; admission; *Eintritt verboten!* no admittance!; *Eintritt frei!* admission free!

einverstanden B *(past. part.)* agreed; all right; *einverstanden sein* agree

Einzelheit D -en *f* detail

einzeln A *(adj.)* single; one by one

einzig A *(adj.)* only; sole; single

Eis C -es *n* ice; ice-cream

Eisen B -s, - *n* iron

elektrisch C *(adj.)* electric(al); *elektrischer Strom* electric current

Eltern B *(pl.)* parents *(pl.)*

empfangen D ä/i/a receive; get

empfinden D i/a/u feel; be sensible of

Ende A -s, -n *n* end; *zu dem Ende* to that purpose; *am Ende* at the end; *zu Ende gehen* come to an end

enden B *(w.v.)* finish; come to an end

endlich A *(adv.)* at last; finally; at length

eng A *(adj.)* narrow; tight; *enge Freunde* intimate friends

England D -s *n* England

Engländer D -s, - *m* Englishman

englisch D *(adj.)* English; *auf englisch* in English; *auf gut englisch* in plain English

entdecken D *(w.v.)* discover; detect

entfernt C *(adj.)* removed; distant; away; (far) off; *5 Kilometer entfernt* 5 kilometres off/away

Entfernung D -en *f* distance

entgegen B *(prep.)* contrary to

entgegengesetzt D *(adj.)* opposite; contrary; *im entgegengesetzten Fall* in the contrary case

entlang B *(prep.)* along

entscheiden C **ei/ie/ie** decide; determine; *sich entscheiden* make up one's mind

[sich] entschließen C **ie/o/o** decide; make up one's mind; *er hat sich anders entschlossen* he has changed his mind

entschlossen D *(adj.)* determined

Entschluß C **-ses, ⁻se** *m* decision; resolution; *einen Entschluß fassen* make up one's mind

entschuldigen C *(w.v.)* excuse; pardon; *entschuldigen Sie!* I beg your pardon!

entstehen D **e/a/a** (a)rise; begin; come into being

entwickeln D *(w.v)* 1. unroll. 2. develop; *einen Film entwickeln* develop a film

Entwicklung D **-en** *f* development

er A *(pers. pron.)* he

erblicken D *(w.v.)* catch sight of

Erde A **-n** *f* earth; world; ground, soil

Ereignis C **-ses, -se** *n* event; incident

erfahren B **ä/u/a** hear; learn; experience; come to know

Erfahrung D **-en** *f* experience; knowledge

Erfolg B **-es, -e** *m* success; achievement; *Erfolg haben* succeed

Ergebnis B **-ses, -se** *n* result; outcome

ergreifen B **ei/i/i** seize; get hold of; catch; *ergriffen sein* be moved

erhalten A **ä/ie/a** receive; get; maintain; *schlecht erhalten* in bad condition

[sich] erholen D *(w.v.)* recover; gain strength

erinnern [an] C *(w.v.)* remind [of]; mention; draw attention to; *wenn ich mich recht erinnere* if I remember rightly

sich erinnern [an] C *(w.v.)* remember; *ich erinnere mich daran, daß* I remember that

Erinnerung D **-en** *f* memory; recollection; *zur Erinnerung* in memory

sich erkälten C *(w.v.)* catch (a) cold

erkennen A **e/a/a** recognize; understand; realize

erklären A *(w.v.)* explain; state; declare

Erklärung B **-en** *f* explanation; statement; declaration

erlauben C *(w.v.)* allow; permit

Erlaubnis D **-se** *f* permission; leave; *um Erlaubnis bitten* beg leave

ernst A *(adj.)* serious; earnest; grave

Ernte B **-n** *f* harvest; crop

erreichen B *(w.v.)* reach; get; achieve; *ein hohes Alter erreichen* live to a great age

erscheinen B **ei/ie/ie** appear; turn up; *es erscheint möglich* it seems possible

ersetzen D *(w.v.)* replace; substitute

erst A *(adv.)* first; only; *der erste beste* the first that comes, anything; *in erster Linie* first of all; *erst ... dann* first ... then; *erst morgen* not until tomorrow; *er ist erst 10* he is only 10

erstaunen D *(w.v.)* astonish; be astonished/surprised

erwähnen C *(w.v.)* mention

erwarten C *(w.v.)* wait for; expect (from); await

erwerben C **i/a/o** acquire; gain

erzählen A *(w.v.)* tell; *man erzählt sich* people say

erzeugen D *(w.v.)* manufacture; produce; *das Erzeugnis* the product; *deutsches Erzeugnis* made in Germany

erziehen B **ie/o/o** bring up; educate

es A *(pers. pron.)* it

essen A **i/a/e** eat; have one's meal; *zu Abend essen* have dinner

Essen B **-s, -** *n* food; meal; *das Essen kochen* cook the meal

etwa B *(adv.)* about; nearly; perhaps

etwas A *(pron.)* something; a bit/little

euch A *(pron.)* you

euer, eure A *(poss. adj. and pron.)* your; yours

F

Fabrik C -en *f* factory; works

Fach D -s, ⁼er *n* compartment; field; line; *in welchem Fach ist er?* what is his occupation?, what's his line?

Faden B -s, ⁼ *m* thread; *den Faden verlieren* lose the thread

fähig [zu] B *(adj.)* capable [of], able [to]; *sie ist zu allem fähig* she is capable of anything

Fahne D -n *f* flag; standard; *mit fliegenden Fahnen* with flying colours

fahren A ä/u/a go; drive; ride; sail; *etwas fahren lassen* let go, give up; *rechts fahren* drive on the right

Fahrer B -s, - *m* driver

Fahrkarte B -n *f* ticket; *einfache Fahrkarte* single ticket

Fahrrad B -s, ⁼er *n* bicycle; bike

Fahrschule D -n *f* driving school

Fahrt C -en *f* drive; journey; ride; trip

Fall C -es, ⁼e *m* 1. fall; *zu Fall bringen* bring down. 2. case; *auf keinen Fall* by no means

fallen A ä/ie/a fall; drop; *im Felde fallen* be killed in action

falls C *(conj.)* if; in case

falsch A *(adj.)* false; wrong; *falsches Spiel* foul play; *falsch verbunden!* sorry, wrong number!

falten D *(w.v.)* fold; *einmal falten* fold in two; *die Hände falten* join/fold one's hands

Familie A -n *f* family; *es liegt in der Familie* it runs in the family

fand → **finden**

fangen A ä/i/a catch; capture; *Feuer fangen* catch fire

Farbe B -n *f* colour; paint

fassen A *(w.v.)* take hold of; seize; catch; *bei der Hand fassen* take by the hand; *einen Entschluß fassen* reach a decision

fast A *(adv.)* almost; nearly

faul C *(adj.)* lazy; idle

Faust D ⁼e *f* fist

Feder D -n *f* spring; pen; feather

fegen D *(w.v.)* sweep

fehlen A *(w.v.)* 1. be absent/lacking/missing; *mir fehlt eine Feder* I need a pen. 2. *was fehlt Ihnen?* what's the matter with you?, what's wrong with you?

Fehler A -s, - *m* mistake; fault; *einen Fehler begehen/ machen* make a mistake

feiern C *(w.v.)* celebrate; be idle

fein A *(adj.)* fine; choice; first-class

Feind C -es, -e *m* enemy

Feld B -es, -er *n* field; *ins Felde führen* bring up; *aus dem Felde schlagen* defeat

Fell D -es, -e *n* skin; fur; hide; *ein dickes Fell haben* be thick-skinned

Fenster A -s, - *n* window

Ferien C *(pl.)* vacation, holidays; *Ferien machen* take one's holidays/vacation

fern B *(adj.)* far; distant; remote; *von fern* from afar

Ferne D -n *f* distance; *aus der Ferne* from a distance

ferner B *(adv.)* further(more); moreover; *fernerhin* for the future

Ferngespräch D -s, -e *n* phone-call; long-distance call

Fernsehen B -s *n* television; *fernsehen* watch television

Fernsprecher D -s, - *m* telephone

fertig A *(adj.)* ready; finished; done

Fest C -es, -e *n* feast; festival; party; *ein Fest begehen* keep a festival

fest A *(adj.)* firm; solid; fixed; *fest überzeugt sein* be fully convinced

festhalten B ä/ie/a hold (tight); hold fast; *sich festhalten (an)* hold on (to), cling (to)

festmachen A *(w.v.)* attach; fasten; fix

feststellen D *(w.v.)* establish; find (out); ascertain

fett B *(adj.)* fat; greasy; *fett machen* fatten

feucht B *(adj.)* moist; damp

Feuer A -s, - *n* fire; *Feuer (an)machen/anzünden* make/ light a fire

Fieber D -s, - *n* fever

fiel → **fallen**

Film A -es, -e *m* film, picture

finden A i/a/u find; *es wird sich finden* we shall see

Finger A -s, - *m* finger; *lange Finger haben* steal

finster B *(adj.)* dark; *finster aussehen* look grim

Firma, C **Firmen** *f* firm; house; company

Fisch B -es, -e *m* fish

flach B *(adj.)* flat; plain; even; level; *flach machen* flatten

Flamme D -n *f* flame; passion; *in Flammen* in flames

Flasche B -n *f* bottle; *eine Flasche Wein* a bottle of wine

Fleisch D -es *n* meat; flesh; *Fleisch ansetzen* grow fat

Fleiß D -es *m* industry; pains *(pl.); fleißig* industrious

Fliege D -n *f* fly; *zwei Fliegen mit einer Klappe schlagen* kill two birds with one stone

fliegen D ie/o/o fly; travel by air

fliehen C ie/o/o flee; escape

fließen B ie/o/o flow; run; *fließend sprechen* speak fluently; *fließendes Wasser* running water

Flucht C *f* flight; escape; *die Flucht ergreifen* flee, take flight

Flüchtling D -s, -e *m* fugitive; refugee

Flug C -es,⸚e *m* flight; flying; *Flugplatz* airport

Flügel D -s, - *m* wing; grand piano

Flugzeug D -es, -e *n* aeroplane; plane

Fluß B -sses,⸚sse *m* river

flüssig B *(adj.)* liquid

Folge C -n *f* sequel; result; consequence; *in der Folge* in future, subsequently

folgen A *(w.v.)* follow; succeed; result from

fordern A *(w.v.)* demand; ask; claim; *zu viel fordern* overcharge

Form A -en *f* shape; form; design

Forscher D -s, - *m* scientist; research worker

fort A *(adv.)* away; forward; *und so fort* and so on

fortfahren B **ä/u/a** keep on; continue; go on

Fortschritt C **-es, -e** *m* progress; improvement; *Fortschritte machen* advance, make progress

fortsetzen C *(w.v.)* continue; pursue

Fortsetzung C **-en** *f* pursuit; sequel; *Fortsetzung folgt!* to be continued!

Foto A **-s, -s** *n* photo; picture

fotografieren B *(w.v.)* photograph; take pictures

Frage A **-n** *f* question; *eine Frage stellen* ask a question; *eine Frage beantworten* answer a question; *das ist keine Frage* that's beyond question

fragen A *(w.v.)* ask; *nach dem Weg fragen* ask one's way; *es fragt sich ob* it is a question whether; *Kaffee ist sehr gefragt* coffee is very much in demand

Frankreich D **-s** *n* France

Franzose D **-n, -n** *m* Frenchman; *die Franzosen* the French

französisch C *(adj.)* French

Frau A **-en** *f* woman; wife; *Frau A* Mrs A

Fräulein A **-s, -** *n* young lady; *Fräulein B* Miss B

frei A *(adj.)* free; vacant; *unter freiem Himmel* in the open air; *Eintritt frei* admission free; *einen Tag frei bekommen* get a day off

Freiheit B **-en** *f* freedom; liberty

freilich C *(adv.)* certainly; indeed

Freizeit D *f* leisure; spare time

fremd B *(adj.)* strange; foreign; unknown

Fremde B **-n, -n** *m* stranger, foreigner

fressen D **i/a/e** eat, devour; *Vieh zu fressen geben* feed the cattle

Freude D **-n** *f* joy; delight; pleasure; *mit Freuden* gladly, with pleasure

freudig C *(adj.)* joyful; glad; cheerful

sich freuen B *(w.v.)* be pleased with; be glad of; *es freut mich sehr* I'm very happy/glad

Freund A **-es, -e** *m* friend; pal; acquaintance; boy-friend

freundlich A *(adj.)* friendly; kind(ly)

Frieden B -s *m* peace; *den Frieden bewahren* keep the peace; *laß mich in Frieden!* leave me alone!

frieren A **ie/o/o** freeze; be/feel cold; *mich friert* I am/feel cold

frisch A *(adj.)* fresh; cool

froh A *(adj.)* glad; cheerful; joyful; *über etwas froh sein* be glad of/about something

fröhlich A *(adj.)* happy; merry; cheerful; *Fröhliche Weihnachten!* Merry Christmas!

Frucht D **ᵘe** *f* fruit

früh A *(adj.)* early

früher A *(adj. comp.)* earlier; sooner; *früher oder später* sooner or later

Frühling C -s, -e *m* spring

Frühstück B -s *n* breakfast; *frühstücken* have breakfast

fühlen A *(w.v.)* feel; touch

fuhr → **fahren**

führen A *(w.v.)* lead; guide; drive; direct; *hinters Licht führen* deceive

Führerschein C -s, -e *m* driving licence

füllen C *(w.v.)* fill; *eine Lücke füllen* stop a gap

Funk D -s *m* wireless; radio; spark

für A *(prep.)* for; in exchange for; instead of; on behalf of; in favour of; for the sake of

Furcht D *f* fear; anxiety; fright; *Furcht haben* be afraid; *aus Furcht vor* from/for fear of

furchtbar C *(adj.)* terrible; awful; fearful

fürchten B *(w.v.)* fear; dread; *sich fürchten vor* be afraid of

Fuß A -es, **ᵘe** *m* foot; *zu Fuß* on foot; *zu Fuß gehen* walk; *vom Kopf bis [zum] Fuß* from top to toe

Fußball C -s, **ᵘe** *m* football; US: soccer;

füttern D *(w.v.)* feed

G

gab → **geben**

Gabe D -n *f* gift; present

Gabel B -n *f* fork

Gang D -es, ⁻e *m* going; walking; walk; gear; speed; *in vollem Gang* in full activity; *in Gang bringen* get going

ganz A *(adj.)* all; whole; wholly; quite; entirely; *ganze zehn Tage* full ten days; *ein ganzer Mann* every inch a man; *ganz und gar* altogether

gar nicht B *(adv.)* not at all

gar nichts C nothing at all

Gardine D -n *f* curtain

Garten B -s, ⁻ *m* garden

Gas C -es, -e *n* gas; *Gas geben* step on the gas/accelerator

Gast C -es, ⁻e *m* guest; *Gäste haben* have guests

Gasthaus D -es, ⁻er *n* inn; restaurant; pub

Gebäude B -s, - *n* building; structure

geben A i/a/e give; *es gibt* there is/are; *was gibt's?* what is the matter?

Gebiet C -es, -e *n* area; district; field; sphere; *auf seinem Gebiet* in his field

gebildet D *(adj.)* educated; well-bred; cultured

Gebirge C -s, - *n* mountains *(pl.)*

geboren C *(past. part.)* born; *geborener Deutscher* German by birth; *geboren werden* be born

Gebrauch C -s, ⁻e *m* use; employment; *im Gebrauch* in use

gebrauchen A *(w.v.)* use; make use (of); employ; *das ist nicht zu gebrauchen* that is of no use; *gebraucht* used, second-hand

Geburt D -en *f* birth; *Geburtsort und -tag* place and date of birth

Geburtstag C -s, -e *m* birthday

Gedächtnis D -ses *n* memory; *aus dem Gedächtnis* by heart; *zum Gedächtnis* [*an*] in memory [of]

Gedanke B -ns, -n *m* thought; idea; *mir kam der Gedanke* the thought struck me

Gedicht D -es, -e *n* poem

Geduld D *f* patience; *Geduld haben* have patience; *die Geduld verlieren* lose patience

geehrter D *(adj.)* : *(sehr) geehrter Herr!* (Dear) Sir,

Gefahr B -en *f* danger; risk; *in Gefahr* in danger; *außer Gefahr* out of danger; *die Gefahr laufen* run the risk

gefährlich B *(adj.)* dangerous

gefallen B ä/ie/a please; *es gefällt mir* I like it; *wie hat ihm das Buch gefallen?* how did he like the book; *wie gefällt Ihnen?* how do you like?

Gefängnis D -ses, -se *n* prison; jail

Gefühl B -s, -e *n* feeling; sentiment

gegen A *(prep.)* towards; against; versus; by; about; compared with

Gegend B -en *f* règion; part; quarter; *in welcher Gegend?* where abouts?

gegeneinander D *(adv.)* against one another/each other

Gegenstand B -s, ⸚e *m* object; item; affair; *zum Gegenstand haben* bear upon

Gegenteil C -s *n* contrary; opposite; *im Gegenteil* on the contrary

gegenüber C *(adv.)* opposite; facing

Gegenwart C *f* presence

gegenwärtig D 1. *(adj.)* present; actual. 2. *(adv.)* at present; nowadays

Gegner D -s, - *m* adversary; enemy; opponent

Gehalt D -s, ⸚er *n* salary; pay; *mit vollem Gehalt* on full pay

geheim D *(adj.)* secret

gehen A e/i/a go; walk; *wie geht es Ihnen?* how are you? *wie geht's ihm?* how is he?

gehorchen C *(w.v.)* obey

gehören [zu] A *(w.v.)* belong [to]; *das gehört dir* that's yours; *das gehört sich nicht* that is not suitable

Geist B **-es, -er** *m* mind; spirit; *der Heilige Geist* the Holy
Ghost

gelb A *(adj.)* yellow

Geld A **-es, -er** *n* money; change; *Geld verdienen* make
money; *flüssiges Geld* ready money

Gelegenheit A **-en** *f* occasion; opportunity; chance; *die
Gelegenheit ergreifen* seize the opportunity; *die Gelegenheit bietet sich* the opportunity presents itself

gelehrt D *(adj.)* learned

gelingen B **i/a/u** succeed in; manage; *es gelingt ihm, es
zu tun* he succeeds in doing it

gelten B **i/a/o** be worth; be effective; *gelten für* be con-
sidered as; *es gilt nicht* it doesn't count

gemäß C *(prep.)* according to

gemein C *(adj.)* common; general; vulgar; base; *eine
gemeine Lüge* a dirty lie

Gemüse C **-s** *n* vegetables

gemütlich D *(adj.)* good-natured; pleasant

genau A *(adj.)* just; exact; exactly; accurately; *ich weiß
es ganz genau* I'm sure of it

genießen C **ie/o/o** enjoy

genommen → **nehmen**

genug A *(adj.)* enough; *genug davon!* no more of this!

genügen B *(w.v.)* be enough; suffice

Gepäck C **-s** *n* luggage; baggage

gerade A 1. *(adj.)* straight; even. 2. *(adv.)* just; exactly;
es ist gerade 2 Uhr it's 2 o'clock sharp; *nun gerade*
now more than ever

Gerät D **-es, -e** *n* instrument; apparatus; set; tool

Geräusch C **-es, -e** *n* noise

gerecht D *(adj.)* just; fair; *eine gerechte Sache* a just cause

Gericht D **-s, -e** *n* law-court; dish

gering A *(adj.)* little; small; low; *geringe Qualität* inferior quality

gern A *(adv.)* gladly; with pleasure; *das glaube ich gern*
I can easily believe that; *er sagte gern* he used to say

Geruch C -s,⁼e *m* smell; scent

Gesang D -s,⁼e *m* song

Geschäft C -s, -e *n* shop; firm; business; *ein gutes Geschäft machen* make a good bargain *Geschäfte machen* do business

geschehen A ie/a/e happen; occur; come about; *geschehen lassen* allow; *was ist geschehen?* what's the matter?, what has happened?

Geschenk B -s, -e *n* gift; present

Geschichte B -n *f* history; story; event; *eine schöne Geschichte* a pretty mess

geschlossen → **schließen**

Geschmack C -s *m* taste

geschrieben → **schreiben**

Geschwindigkeit C -en *f* speed; *mit einer Geschwindigkeit von* at a rate/speed of

Gesellschaft C -en *f* society; company; party; *in guter Gesellschaft* in good company; *eine Gesellschaft geben* give a party

Gesetz D -es, -e *n* law

Gesicht A -s, -er *n* face; *ins Gesicht sehen* face, look in the face; *aus dem Gesicht verlieren* lose sight of

Gespräch B -s, -e *n* conversation; talk; *sich in ein Gespräch einlassen* enter into conversation; *ein Gespräch führen (mit)* have a talk (with)

gesprochen → **sprechen**

Gestalt C -en *f* figure; form, shape; *in Gestalt von* in the shape of

gestehen D e/a/a admit; confess; *um die Wahrheit zu gestehen* to tell the truth

gestern A *(adv.)* yesterday; *gestern abend* last night

gestorben [→**sterben**] C *(past part.)* dead

gesund A *(adj.)* healthy; sound; well; *frisch und gesund* safe and sound; *gesund werden* recover; *gesund machen* cure

getan → **tun**

Getränk D -s, -e *n* drink

Getreide D -s *n* cereals *(pl.)*; corn

gewähren D *(w.v.)* grant; allow

Gewalt B -en *f* power; might; force; *mit Gewalt* by force

gewandt D *(adj.)* skilled; skilful; *gewandt sein in* be good at

Gewehr D -s, -e *n* gun; rifle

gewesen –> **sein**

Gewicht C -s, -e *n* weight; *an Gewicht verlieren* lose weight

Gewinn C -s, -e *m* gain; profit; prize

gewinnen A i/a/o gain; win; *einen Preis gewinnen* win a prize; *vier zu drei gewinnen* win by 4 goals to 3

gewiß A 1. *(adj.)* certain; sure. 2. *(adv.)* certainly; surely, *aber gewiß!* why certainly!, but of course!

Gewissen D -s *n* conscience

sich gewöhnen [an] D *(w.v.)* get accustomed/used [to]; *gewöhnt sein* be used [to]

Gewohnheit B -en *f* habit; custom; use; *aus Gewohnheit* by/from habit; *zur Gewohnheit werden* grow into a habit

gewöhnlich A *(adj.)* general; ordinary; usual

geworden –> **werden**

gib, gibt –> **geben**

gießen A ie/o/o pour; water; *es gießt* it is raining cats and dogs; *die Blumen gießen* water the flowers

Gift D -es, -e *n* poison

ging –> **gehen**

Gipfel D -s, - *m* top; summit; peak

glänzen C *(w.v.)* shine; flash; *glänzend* bright; brilliant

Glas B -es, ⁼er *n* glass; *gefärbtes Glas* stained glass; *ein Glas Bier* a glass of beer

glatt A *(adj.)* smooth; polished; slippery; *alles ging glatt* everything went smoothly

Glaube D -ns *m* faith; belief

glauben A *(w.v.)* think; believe; *ich glaube schon* I suppose so; *glaubst du?* do you think so?

gleich A *(adj.)* equal; same; like; similar; *gleich machen* level, equalize; *das ist mir gleich* it's all the same to me; *von gleichem Alter* of the same age

gleich A *(adv.)* 1. equally; alike. 2. at once; in a moment; *gleich als* as soon as; *gleich als ob* just as if

gleichfalls C *(adv.)* also; as well; *danke gleichfalls!* thanks, the same to you!

Gleichheit D *f* equality

gleichzeitig C *(adj. and adv.)* simultaneous; at the same time

Glied D -es, -er *n* limb; member

Glocke C -n *f* bell; *die Glocken läuten* ring the bells

Glück B -s *n* [good] luck; chance; fortune; *kein Glück haben* be out of luck; *viel Glück!* good luck!

glücklich B *(adj.)* lucky; happy; *glückliche Reise!* have a pleasant trip! *er ist glücklich angekommen* he arrived safely

Gold B -es *n* gold; *aus Gold* made of gold

Gott D -es, ⁔er *m* God; *Gott sei dank!* thank God!; *in Gottes Namen!* for Heaven's sake!

graben B ä/u/a dig

Grad C -es, -e *m* degree; rank; *in dem Grade, daß* to such an extend that; *in höchstem Grade* exceedingly

Gramm C -s, - *n* gram(me)

Gras D -es, ⁔er *n* grass; *ins Gras beißen* bite the dust

grau A *(adj.)* grey

greifen A ei/i/i seize; catch; reach for

Grenze C -n *f* frontier; border; limit; *an der Grenze* on the frontier; *seine Geduld hat bald ihre Grenze erreicht* he has almost reached the limit of his patience

Griff D -s, -e *m* grip; handle; *ein glücklicher Griff* a lucky hit

grob C *(adj.)* coarse; rough; raw; *in groben Zügen* approximately, roughly; *ein grober Fehler* a bad mistake

groß A *(adj.)* great; large; big; tall; *im großen* on a large scale; *mit großer Mühe* with great pains; *große Ferien* summer vacation; *er ist sehr groß* he is very tall

großartig B *(adj.)* great; splendid; first-rate; wonderful

Größe B -n *f* size; height
Großmutter C⁼ *f* grandmother
Großvater C -s,⁼ *m* grandfather
größtenteils D *(adv.)* largely; for the most part; mostly
grün A *(adj.)* green
Grund A -es, ⁼e *m* ground; bottom; cause; reason; *auf den Grund gehen* get to the bottom of; *zu Grunde gehen* be ruined; *aus welchem Grund?* for what reason?, why?
Grundsatz D -es,⁼e *m* principle
Gruppe C -n *f* group; team
Gruß B -es,⁼e *m* greeting; regards *(pl.)*; *mit bestem Gruß* sincerely yours;
grüßen C *(w.v.)* greet; *grüßen Sie Ihre Mutter von mir* remember me to your mother
gucken A *(w.v.)* look; peep
Gummi B -s, -s *m* gum; rubber
günstig C *(adj.)* favourable; *im günstigsten Fall* at best, at most
gut A *(adj.)* good; well; all right; *kurz und gut* in short; *schon gut!* never mind!; *alles gute!* have a nice time!, good luck; *für gut halten* think fit
Gut D -es,⁼er *n* property; farm; estate

H

Haar A -es, -e *n* hair; *sich die Haare schneiden lassen* have one's hair cut
haben A *(w.v.)* have; have got; *im Auge haben* have in sight; *gern haben* like, be fond of; *unrecht haben* be wrong; *an sich haben* be wearing
Hafen B -s,⁼ *m* port; harbour.
Hahn B -s,⁼e *m* cock; rooster; tap; *der Hahn kräht* the cock crows; *den Hahn zudrehen* turn off the tap
halb A *(adj.)* half; *eine halbe Stunde* half an hour; *halb drei (Uhr)* half past two; *5 nach halb drei* twenty-five to three; *anderthalb* one and a half

Hälfte - Haus H

Hälfte B **-n** *f* half
Halle B **-n** *f* hall
Hals A **-es,** **⸚e** *m* neck; throat; *einen bösen Hals haben* have a sore throat
Halt! A *(interj.)* stop!
halten A **ä/ie/a** hold; keep; possess; stop; *eine Rede halten* make a speech; *sich gut halten* behave well; *wofür halten Sie mich?* what do you take me for?; *der Bus hält* the bus stops
Haltung D **-en** *f* attitude
Hammer B **-s,** **⸚** *m* hammer
Hand A **⸚e** *f* hand; *an die Hand gehen* aid, help; *bei der Hand* at hand
Handel C **-s** *m* trade; commerce; *Handel treiben* do business; trade
Handlung D **-en** *f* action; act; (often in compound = shop) *Buchhandlung* book-shop
Handschuh D **-s, -e** *m* glove; *ein Paar Handschuhe* a pair of gloves
Handtuch C **-s,** **⸚er** *n* towel
Handwerk D **-s, -e** *n* trade; craft; *sein Handwerk verstehen* know one's business
hängen A **ä/i/a** hang; attach
hart A *(adj.)* hard; firm; solid; rough; severe; *harte Worte* harsh words *(pl.)*; *hart werden* harden, grow hard
hassen C *(w.v.)* hate
häßlich C *(adj.)* ugly; nasty; mean
hast, hat → **haben**
häufig A 1. *(adj.)* frequent. 2. *(adv.)* frequently; often
Haupt B **-es,** **⸚er** *n* head; chief
Hauptsache B **-n** *f* main point/thing; most important thing; *das ist die Hauptsache* that is all that matters
Hauptstadt D **⸚e** *f* capital
Haus A **-es,** **⸚er** *n* house; home; *außer dem Hause* out of doors; *nach Hause gehen* go home; *zu Hause sein* be at home, be in; *von zu Hause* not at home

Haut C⁓e *f* skin; hide; *eine dicke Haut haben* be thick-skinned; *nur Haut und Knochen* nothing but skin and bones

heben A e/o/o lift; raise; *heben und senken* rise and fall

Heer D -es, -e *n* army

Heft B -es, -e *n* exercise-book; note-book

heftig B *(adj.)* violent; strong; intense; *heftig werden* get into a temper

heilen D *(w.v.)* cure; heal

heilig D *(adj.)* holy; sacred; *Heiliger Abend* Christmas Eve

Heim B -s, -e *n* home; dwelling

Heimat C *f* native country/place; home; *in die Heimat zurückfahren* return home

heimkehren D *(w.v.)* come back; return home

heiraten C *(w.v.)* marry; get married

heiß A *(adj.)* hot; *mir ist heiß* I feel/am hot; *kochend heiß* boiling hot;

heißen A ei/ie/ei call; name; mean; be called; *es heißt* it is said; *er heißt Hans* his name is Hans; *was soll das heißen?* what does [all] that mean?

heiter C *(adj.)* bright; cheerful, gay; *heiter werden* cheer up

heizen B *(w.v.)* heat; fire up; make a fire

helfen A i/a/o help; serve; *was hilft es?* what's the use of it?;

hell A *(adj.)* bright; clear; light; *am hellen Tag* in broad daylight; *die helle Wahrheit* the plain truth

Hemd B -es, -en *n* shirt;

her B *(adv.)* here; *komm her!* come here!; *wo kommen Sie her?* where do you come from?; *von je her* always; *wie lang ist das her?* how long ago was that?

herauf B *(adv.)* up; upwards; *die Treppe herauf* upstairs

heraus A *(adv.)* out; out here; *heraus!* get out!; *heraus mit der Sprache!* speak up!

Herbst D -es, -e *m* autumn; fall; *im Herbst* in autumn

Herd C -es, -e *m* fireplace; stove

herein A *(adv.)* in; into; *herein!* come in!

hereinkommen B o/a/o come in(side); enter

Herr A **-n, -en** *m* gentleman; master; *mein Herr!* sir!; *Herr X* Mr X

herrlich D *(adj.)* grand; wonderful; splendid

herrschen D *(w.v.)* rule; reign

herstellen B *(w.v.)* produce; make

herum B *(adv.)* (a)round; about; *rund/rings herum* all/ round about; *um den Tisch herum* around the table

herunter B *(adv.)* down; downward; *gerade herunter* straight down

hervorragend D *(adj.)* distinguished; excellent

Herz A **-ens, -en** *n* heart; *Hand aufs Herz!* truly!; *im Herzen der Stadt* in the centre of the city; *ohne Herz* heartless; *von ganzem Herzen* with all my heart

herzlich B *(adj.)* cordial; affectionate; *herzlich gern* readily, with pleasure

heute A *(adv.)* today; this day; *bis heute* till today; *noch heute* this very day; *heute morgen* this morning

heutzutage D *(adv.)* nowadays; in these days

hielt → **halten**

hier A *(adv.)* here; *hier bin ich* here I am

hierauf D *(adv.)* upon this; then, after this

hierher A *(adv.)* here, this way; *hierher!* come here; *bis hierher* up to now, so far

Hilfe B **-n** *f* help; aid; support; *Hilfe!* help!; *erste Hilfe* first aid;

Himmel A **-s, -** *m* sky; heaven; *unter freiem Himmel* in the open air; *zwischen Himmel und Erde* between heaven and earth; *du lieber Himmel!* Good God!

hin A *(adv.)* there; *hin und her* to and fro; *er ist hin* he is dead

hinauf B *(adv.)* up; upward(s); *da hinauf* up there; *die Treppe hinauf* upstairs

hinaus B *(adv.)* out; outside; *hinaus!* (get) out;

hinausgehen B e/i/a go out; leave

hindern D *(w.v.)* hinder; stop; check; prevent (from)

hindurch D *(adv.)* through; during; *den ganzen Tag hindurch* all day [long]

hinein A *(adv.)* in, into; inside

hinfallen C **ä/ie/a** fall (down); *hinfallen lassen* drop

hinlegen A *(w.v.)* lay/put down; *sich hinlegen* lie down, go to bed

hinten B *(adv.)* behind; after; *nach hinten* backwards

hinter A *(prep.)* behind; after; *hinter mir* behind me

hintereinander D *(adv.)* one after the other; *vier Tage hintereinander* four days running

hinterher C *(adv.)* behind; after; afterwards

hinunter B *(adv.)* down; downwards; downstairs

hinzufügen D *(w.v.)* add; enclose

Hitze B *f* heat

hoch A *(adj.)* high; tall; *Kopf hoch!* cheer up!

höchst D *(adv.)* highly; extremely; *es ist höchste Zeit* it is high time

höchstens B *(adv.)* at [the] most/best

Hof B **-es, ⸚e** *m* court; yard; farm

hoffen B *(w.v.)* hope; *ich hoffe es* I hope so

hoffentlich B *(adj.)* it is to be hoped; as I hope; let's hope

Hoffnung C **-en** *f* hope; expectation

höflich C *(adj.)* polite

Höhe C **-n** *f* height

hohl D *(adj.)* hollow; *ein hohler Baum* a hollow tree

holen A *(w.v.)* fetch; get; go/come for; *holen lassen* send for; *Atem holen* draw breath

Holz B **-es, ⸚er** *n* wood; timber; *aus Holz* [made] of wood

Honig D **-s** *m* honey

hören A *(w.v.)* hear; listen; *hören Sie auf!* stop it!; *hören Sie mal!* I say!; *hören Sie zu!* listen!; *von sich hören lassen* let know, send word

Hörer C **-s, -** *m* listener; (telephone) receiver; *den Hörer abnehmen/auflegen* lift/replace the receiver

Hose A **-n** *f* trousers *(pl.)*; pants *(pl.)*; *eine Hose* a pair of trousers

Hotel B -s, -s *n* hotel

hübsch A *(adj.)* pretty; nice; beautiful; *das war hübsch von Ihnen* that was nice of you; *ganz hübsch* rather nice/pretty

Hügel D -s, - *m* hill

Huhn B -s, ⁻er *n* chicken; hen; *Hühner* poultry

Hund B -es, -e *m* dog; hound; *auf den Hund kommen* go to the dogs; *Vorsicht, Bissiger Hund!* beware of the dog!

hundert A *(card.)* a/one hundred

Hunger A -s *m* hunger; *Hunger haben* be hungry; *Hungers sterben* starve to death

hungrig B *(adj.)* hungry

husten C *(w.v.)* cough; *den Husten haben* have a cough

Hut A -s,⁻e *m* hat; *den Hut abnehmen* take off one's hat; *mit dem Hut in der Hand* hat in hand

sich hüten [vor] D *(w.v.)* guard [against]; watch/look out for; *hüten Sie sich!* keep off!

Hütte D -n *f* hut; cottage; *Eisenhütte* iron-foundry

I

ich A *(pers. pron.)* I; *ich selbst* I myself; *sein liebes ich* his own dear self

ideal C *(adj.)* ideal; perfect

Ideal D -s, -e *n* ideal; model

Idee A -n *f* idea; concept

ihm A *(pers. pron.)* [to] him/it

ihn A *(pers. pron.)* him, it

ihr A *(pers. pron.)* you; [to] her

ihr [-e] A *(poss. adj.)* her; their

ihre [-r, -s] A *(pron.)* hers; theirs

Ihr [-e] A *(poss. adj. and pron.)* your, yours

im = **in dem**

immer A *(adv.)* always; every time; *immer mehr* more and more; *immer noch* still; *auf immer* for ever

immerhin D *(adv.)* after all; nevertheless

in A *(prep.)* in; into; , during; within; *in kurzem* shortly; *in aller Frühe* at day-break

indem C *(conj.)* as; while; by;

Industrie C -n *f* industry; *Gewerbe und Industrie* trade and industry

infolge C *(prep.)* in consequence of; owing to; as a result of

Ingenieur B -s, -e *m* engineer

Inhalt B -s, -e *m* contents *(pl.)* *Inhaltsverzeichnis* index, table of contents

innen C *(adv.)* in; within; inside; *von innen* from within; *nach innen* inward(s)

innere D *(adj.)* inner

innerhalb C *(prep.)* within

ins = **in das**

Insekt C -s, -en *n* insect

Insel B -n *f* island; isle;

Instrument C -es, -e *n* instrument; tool; utensil

interessant A *(adj.)* interesting

Interesse B -s, -n *n* interest; *Interesse nehmen* [*an*] take an interest [in]

sich interessieren [**für**] D *(w.v.)* be interested [in]

inzwischen C *(adv.)* meanwhile; in the meantime

irgendein A -er, -e, -es *(pron. and adj.)* some(one); any(one); somebody

irren C *(w.v.)* err; be mistaken/wrong; *sich irren* make a mistake; *wenn ich mich nicht irre* if I'm not mistaken

Irrtum D -s, ̈er *m* error; mistake; *sehr in Irrtum sein* be greatly mistaken; *im Irrtum* in error

ist → **sein**

J

ja A *(adv.)* yes; *da sind Sie ja!* well there you are
Jacke B -n *f* jacket
Jagd D -en *f* hunting; shooting; *auf die Jagd gehen* go hunting/shooting; *Jagd machen* hunt, chase
jagen D *(w.v.)* hunt; chase
Jäger D -s, - *m* hunter
Jahr A -es, -e *n* year; *nächtes/vergangenes Jahr* next/last year; *vor einem Jahr* a year ago
Jahreszeit C -en *f* season
Jahrhundert C -s, -e *n* century
jährlich C *(adj.)* yearly; annually; every year; *einmal jährlich* once a year
je[mals] C *(adv.)* ever; at any time
je . . . desto D the . . . the; *je mehr, desto besser* the more the better
jedenfalls D *(adv.)* in any case; however
jeder A *(pron.)* each; every(body); any(body); *jeder der* whoever; *zu jeder Zeit* at any time
jedermann C *(pron.)* everyone; everybody
jedesmal C *(adv.)* every time; each time
jedoch B *(conj.)* however; yet; nevertheless
jemand A *(pron.)* somebody; anybody; *jemand anders* somebody else
jenseits D *(adv.)* on the other side
jetzt A *(adv.)* now; at present
Jugend A *f* youth; young people
jung A *(adj.)* young
Junge A -n, -n *m* boy

K

Kaffee C -s, -s *m* coffee; *eine Tasse Kaffee* a cup of coffee; *Kaffee kochen* make coffee

kalt A *(adj.)* cold; cool; *mir ist kalt* I am/feel cold

Kälte B *f* cold(ness); *vor Kälte zittern* shiver with cold

kam → **kommen**

Kamera D -s *f* camera

Kamerad A -en, -en *m* comrade; fellow; companion; pal

Kamm C -s, ⸚e *m* comb; *über einen Kamm scheren* treat all alike

[sich] kämmen C *(w.v.)* comb [one's hair]

Kampf C -es, ⸚e *m* fight; struggle; match; *im Kampfe fallen* be killed in action

kämpfen C *(w.v.)* fight; struggle

kann → **können**

Kapitän D -s, -e *m* captain; skipper

kaputt B *(adj.)* broken; in pieces; *kaputtmachen* ruin, break

Karte A -n *f* map; chart; card; ticket; menu; *Karte von Deutschland* map of Germany; *ein Spiel Karten* a pack of cards; *eine Karte lösen* buy a ticket

Kartoffel A -n *f* potato

Käse C -s, - *m* cheese

Kasse C -n *f* money/cash box; box/booking office; *gegen Kasse* for cash

Kasten B -s, ⸚ *m* box; case

Katze D -n *f* cat; *die Katze im Sack kaufen* buy a pig in a poke

kauen C *(w.v.)* chew

Kauf D -s, ⸚e *m* purchase; buying; bargain; *zum Kauf anbieten* offer for sale

kaufen A *(w.v.)* buy; purchase; *billig kaufen* buy cheap; *teuer kaufen* buy dear

kaum A *(adv.)* hardly; scarcely; *kaum . . . als* no sooner . . . than

kehren D *(w.v.)* sweep; turn; *alles zum besten kehren* turn everything to advantage

kein [-e [-r, -s]] A *(adj. and pron.)* no; not a; not any; no one; none; nobody; *keiner von beiden* neither

Keller B -s, - *m* cellar; basement

kennen A e/a/a know; *kennenlernen* get to know, meet
Kenntnis D -se *f* knowledge; *Kenntnis erhalten* hear, learn, be informed of
Kerl D -s, -e *m* fellow
Kilo C -s, - *n* kilo(gram)
Kilometer B -s, - *m* kilometre
Kind A -es, -er *n* child
Kino C -s, -s *n* cinema; *ins Kino gehen* go to the pictures
Kirche C -n *f* church; *in der Kirche* at church; *in die Kirche* to church
Kirsche D -n *f* cherry
Klage D -n *f* complaint
klar A *(adj.)* clear; bright; *klare Antwort* plain answer; *na, klar!* obviously!
Klasse C -n *f* class; order; grade; *erster Klasse* first-class
kleben D *(w.v.)* glue; paste; stick
Kleid A -es, -er *n* dress; frock; *die Kleider* dresses, clothes
Kleidung A -en *f* clothes; clothing
klein A *(adj.)* little; small
klettern D *(w.v.)* climb; mount; scale; *auf einen Berg klettern* scale a mountain
Klinge D -n *f* blade; sword
Klingel C -n *f* alarm; bell; *es klingelt* the bell is ringing
klopfen C *(w.v.)* knock; beat; *es klopft* there is a knock at the door
klug B *(adj.)* clever; intelligent; *klug werden* grow wise; *Klugheit* brains *(pl.)*, cleverness
Knie D -s, - *n* knee
Knochen D -s, - *m* bone
Knopf D -es, ⁼e *m* button; *auf den Knopf drücken* press the button; *einen Knopf annähen* sew on a button
kochen A *(w.v.)* boil; cook; do the cooking; *sie kocht gut* she is a good cook
Koffer C -s, - *m* suit-case; trunk
Kohle B -n *f* coal; *auf glühenden Kohlen sitzen* be on tenterhooks
Kollege D -n, -n *m* colleague

komisch B *(adj.)* comic(al); funny; strange; *er ist ein komischer Kerl* he's a queer fellow

kommen A o/a/o come; *wie kommen Sie dazu?* what makes you think that?; *wie kommt es, daß ...?* how is it that ...?; *aus den Augen kommen* lose sight of; *kommen lassen* send for

Konferenz D -en *f* conference; meeting

können A a/o/o be able to; know; *das kann sein* that may be [so]; *er kann nichts* he doesn't know a thing; *ich kann nichts dafür* I cannot help it; *er kann Deutsch* he knows German

Konzert B -s, -e *n* concert

Kopf A -es, ⸚e *m* head; brains; *aus dem Kopf* by heart; *Kopf hoch!* cheer up!; *auf den Kopf stellen* turn upside down; *er ist ein kluger Kopf* he's got brains

Korn B -s, ⸚er *n* corn; grain; *die Flinte ins Korn werfen* give up

Körper A -s, - *m* body; *der menschliche Körper* the human body; *körperlich* bodily

kostbar B *(adj.)* precious; valuable; expensive

kosten A *(w.v.)* cost; taste; *wie viel kostet es?* how much is it?; *er kostet den Wein* he'll taste the wine

Kosten D *(pl.)* costs *(pl.)*; expenses *(pl.)*; *auf Kosten von* at the expense of; *die Kosten tragen* pay the expenses

Kraft A ⸚e *f* strength; force; power; *in Kraft sein* be in force; *nach besten Kräften* to the best of one's ability

Kraftfahrer D -s, - *m* driver; motorist

kräftig A *(adj.)* strong; powerful

krank A *(adj.)* ill, sick; *krank werden* fall ill

Krankenhaus B -es, ⸚er *n* hospital; *ins Krankenhaus bringen* take to the hospital

Krankheit B -en *f* illness; sickness; disease; *sich eine Krankheit zuziehen* fall ill, be taken ill

Kreide D -n *f* chalk; crayon; *in der Kreide sitzen* be deeply in debt

Kreis A -es, -e *m* circle; ring; sphere; *sich im Kreise drehen* rotate, spin round

Kreuz D -es, -e *n* cross. Note adv. use: *kreuz und quer* criss-cross, in all directions

kriechen D ie/o/o creep; crawl

Krieg B -es, -e *m* war; *im Krieg* at war, in war-time; *Krieg führen* make war

kriegen B *(w.v.)* get; obtain

Kritik D -en *f* criticism; *unter aller Kritik* beneath contempt; *Kritik üben* criticize

krumm B *(adj.)* crooked; curved; arched; *krumme Nase* hooked nose

Küche B -n *f* kitchen; cooking; *bürgerliche Küche* plain cooking

Kuchen D -s, - *m* cake; pastry

Kugel B -n *f* ball; bullet; *sich eine Kugel durch den Kopf jagen* blow out one's brains

Kuh C ⸚e *f* cow

kühl A *(adj.)* cool; chilly

Kultur D -en *f* culture; civilization

Kunde D -n, -n *m* customer, client

Kunst C ⸚e *f* art, *das ist keine Kunst* that's easy

Künstler D -s, - *m* artist

Kunstwerk D -s, -e *n* work of art

Kurs C -es, -e *m* course; rate of exchange; *Kurs nehmen nach* set course for; *einen Kurs besuchen* attend a course

Kurve C -n *f* curve; bend; turn; *scharfe Kurve* sharp turn

kurz A *(adj.)* short; brief; *in kurzem* shortly, soon; *vor kurzem* recently, the other day

kürzlich D *(adv.)* lately; recently

küssen C *(w.v.)* kiss

Küste D -n *f* coast; shore; beach; *die Küste entlang* along the coast

L

lächeln B *(w.v.)* smile; *worüber lächelt er?* what's he smiling at?

lachen A *(w.v.)* laugh; *das ist nicht zum Lachen* that's no laughing matter

Laden C -s,⸚ *m* shop; store

Ladung D -en *f* load; freight; cargo

lag → **liegen**

Lage A -n *f* situation; position, location; *die Lage der Dinge* state of affairs; *eine gespannte Lage* a tense situation

Lager C -s, - *n* stock; supply; camp; couch; *auf Lager* in store/stock

Lampe C -n *f* lamp

Land A -es,⸚er *n* land; country; *an Land gehen* go ashore; *auf dem Lande wohnen* live in the country

Landkarte D -n *f* map

Landstraße C -n *f* road; highroad

Landwirt C -s, -e *m* farmer

Landwirtschaft D *f* agriculture; farming

landen C *(w.v.)* land; touch down; *glücklich landen* make a safe landing

lang A *(adj.)* long; tall; *10 Jahre lang* for 10 years; *sein Leben lang* all his life; *seit langer Zeit* for a long time

lange A *(adv.)* long; a long while; [for] a long time; *sind Sie schon lange hier?* have you been here long?; *lange her* long ago; *lange hin* a long time yet

Länge C -n *f* length; *auf die Länge* in the long run; *in die Länge ziehen* prolong, draw out

längs B *(prep.)* along

langsam A *(adj.)* slow; *langsam fahren* drive slowly

längst D *(adv.)* for a long time; long ago; *schon längst* long ago

langweilig C *(adj.)* boring; dull; *langweilige Person* bore

Lappen C -s, - *m* rag; cloth

Lärm C -s *m* noise; *blinder Lärm* false alarm; *Lärm machen* make noise

lassen A ä/ie/a let; allow; permit; make; *lassen Sie das!* leave it alone; *laß!* stop it!, don't!; *sich Zeit lassen* take one's time; *sich machen lassen* have made, have done; *rufen lassen* send for; *das muß man ihr lassen* you have to grant her that

Last D -en *f* load; cargo; freight

Lauf B -s, ̈e *m* course; race; range; current; *im vollen Laufe* at top speed; *im Laufe der Zeit* in course of time

laufen A äu/ie/au run; walk; go; move; *laufen lassen* let go; *Gefahr laufen* run the risk; *das Wasser läuft* the water flows

Laune C -n *f* humour; *in guter Laune sein* be in good temper

laut A *(adj.)* loud; clear; *laut lesen* read aloud; *laut sprechen* speak up; *mit lauter Stimme* in a loud voice

läuten C *(w.v.)* ring; sound; *es läutet* the bell rings/is ringing

leben B *(w.v.)* live; *genug zu leben haben* have enough to live on; *leben von* live by

Leben B -s *n* life; *am Leben bleiben* survive; *am Leben sein* be alive; *ums Leben bringen* kill

lebendig B *(adj.)* living; alive; lively; *lebendige Farben* bright colours

Lebensmittel C *(pl.)* food, provisions

lebhaft B *(adj.)* lively; gay; *lebhafter Verkehr* heavy traffic

Leder C -s *n* leather; *aus Leder* [made] of leather

ledig D *(adj.)* unmarried; single

leer A *(adj.)* empty; vacant; unoccupied; *mit leeren Händen* empty-handed

leeren B *(w.v.)* empty; *ein Glas leeren* finish [off] a glass

legen A *(w.v.)* put; lay; place; *sich legen* lie down, go to bed

Lehre B -n *f* lesson; instruction; theory; *das soll ihr eine Lehre sein* that is meant to be a warning to her

lehren B *(w.v.)* teach; instruct; *Deutsch lehren* teach German

Lehrer B -s, - *m* teacher; master; instructor

Lehrling D -s, -e *m* apprentice

Leib B -es, -er *m* body; stomach; womb; *am ganzen Leibe zittern* tremble all over

leicht A *(adj.)* light; easy; slight; *es sich leicht machen* take it easy; *das ist leicht möglich* that is quite possible

Leid C -s, -en *n* sorrow; pain; harm; misfortune; *Leid tragen* mourn; *es tut mir leid* I'm sorry

leiden C ei/i/i suffer; stand; *viel zu leiden haben* have a hard time; *Schaden leiden* suffer damage

Leidenschaft C -en *f* passion; emotion; *ein Ausbruch der Leidenschaft* an outburst of passion

leider B *(adv.)* unfortunately; I'm afraid . . .; alas; *leider muß ich gehen* I'm afraid I have to go

leihen B ei/ie/ie lend; borrow; hire; *sich etwas leihen* borrow something

leise A *(adj.)* soft; gentle; low; *bitte leise!* quiet, please!; *mit leiser Stimme* in a low voice

leisten B *(w.v.)* do; work; accomplish; carry out; *Hilfe leisten* lend a hand; *einen Eid leisten* take an oath

Leiter D -n *f* ladder; *eine Leiter besteigen* climb a ladder

Leitung B -en *f* command; management; wire; line; *Leitung besetzt!* the line is engaged/busy!

lernen A *(w.v.)* learn; study; *auswendig lernen* learn by heart; *kennenlernen* get to know; *Deutsch lernen* learn/study German

lesen A ie/a/e read; *laut lesen* read aloud

letzt A *(adj.)* last; latest; *zu guter letzt* finally; *letzten Montag* last Monday; *in letzter Zeit* lately, of late

leuchten C *(w.v.)* [give] light; shine

Leute B *(pl.)* people *(pl.)*; folks *(pl.)*; *gewisse Leute* certain people; *die meisten Leute* most people

Licht A -es, -er *n* light; candle; *bei Licht* in the daylight; *hinters Licht führen* cheat, deceive; *Licht ausschalten* switch off the light

lieb B *(adj.)* dear; *es ist mir lieb* I'm pleased

Liebe B *f* love; *aus Liebe zu* for love of

lieben A *(w.v.)* love; like; be fond of; *sie lieben sich* they love one another

liebenswürdig D *(adj.)* kind, lovable

lieber A dearer; rather; *je länger, je lieber* the longer, the better; *ich möchte lieber* I would rather

Lied A -es, -er *n* song; *ein Lied singen* sing a song

lief → **laufen**

liefern B *(w.v.)* deliver; supply; furnish

liegen A ie/a/e lie; be situated; be placed; be; *krank im Bett liegen* be sick in bed; *an wem liegt es?* whose fault is it?; *wie die Sachen jetzt liegen* as matters now stand

ließ → **lassen**

liest → **lesen**

Lineal D -s, -e *n* ruler

Linie B -n *f* line; *auf der ganzen Linie* all along the line; *in erster Linie* first of all; *in letzter Linie* finally

link B *(adj.)* left

links B *(adv.)* on the left; *links von* to the left of

Lippe B -n *f* lip

Liste C -n *f* list; *eine Liste aufstellen* draw up a list

Liter C -s, - *n* litre

Literatur D -en *f* literature

Loch B -s, ⸚er *n* hole

Löffel B -s, - *m* spoon; *löffelvoll* spoonful

Lohn C -s, ⸚e *m* wages *(pl.)*; salary; pay; *viel Lohn* high wages

Los D -es, -e *n* lot; destiny; lottery ticket

los! B *(interj.)* go on!; go ahead!; fire away!; begin!;

los B *(adj. + adv.)* : *was ist los?* what's the matter?; what's up?; *was ist mit ihm los?* what's the matter with him?

loslassen D ä/ie/a let go; set free; release

lösen B *(w.v.)* loosen; undo; detach; *eine Fahrkarte lösen* buy a ticket; *eine Aufgabe lösen* solve a problem

Luft A ⸚e *f* air; *er hat keine Luft* he is short of breath: *in die Luft springen/sprengen* blow up (intransitive/ transitive)

Luftpost D *f* air mail

Lüge C -n *f* lie; *eine gewaltige Lüge* a big lie

Lust B ⁺e *f* pleasure; desire; joy; *mit Lust und Liebe* with heart and soul; *ich habe keine Lust dazu* I don't want ·to

lustig B *(adj.)* gay; merry; cheerful; funny; *sich lustig machen* [*über*] make fun [of]

M

machen A *(w.v.)* make; produce; do; *sich die Haare machen* dress one's hair; *fertig machen* get ready; *was macht er?* what's he doing?; *nichts zu machen* nothing doing; *mach's gut!* cheerio!

Macht B ⁺e *f* power; force; strength; *an der Macht* in power; *das steht nicht in meiner Macht* that's beyond my power

mächtig C *(adj.)* powerful; mighty; strong; *der deutschen Sprache mächtig sein* have a good command of the German language

Mädchen A -s, - *n* girl; maid

mag → **mögen**

Magen C -s, ⁺ *m* stomach; *mit leerem Magen zu Bett gehen* go to bed on an empty stomach

mager D *(adj.)* thin; lean

Mahlzeit D -en *f* meal

mal C once; just; *sag mal!* I say!; *denk dir mal!* just imagine!; *3 mal 4 ist 12* 3 times 4 are/make 12

Mal C -s, -e *n* time; *zum ersten Mal* for the first time; *das nächste Mal* next time; *dieses eine Mal* just this once

malen B *(w.v.)* paint

Mama A -s *f* mummy

man B *(pron.)* one; you; we; they; people; *man hat mir gesagt* I was told

manche [-r, -s] C *(adj. and pron.)* many a

manchmal A *(adv.)* often; now and again

Mangel C -s, ⁓ *m* lack; absence; want; *aus Mangel an* for want of

Mann A -es, ⁓er *m* man; husband; *der Mann auf der Straße* the man in the street

männlich D *(adj.)* male; masculine

Mantel A -s, ⁓ *m* coat; overcoat; *einen Mantel tragen* wear a coat

Mappe D -n *f* briefcase; file

Mark B *f* mark; *3 Mark* 3 marks

Marke D -n *f* mark; sign; brand; make

Markt C -s, ⁓e *m* market; market-place; *auf den Markt bringen* put on the market

Marsch D -es, ⁓e *m* march; *auf dem Marsch* en route

Maschine B -n *f* machine; engine; *auf der Maschine schreiben* type(-write)

Maß B -es, -e *n* measure; size; *in hohem Maße* to a great extent; *Maß nehmen* take measurements

mäßig D *(adj.)* moderate

Masse C -n *f* mass; *eine Masse Geld* lots of money

Material C -s, -ien *n* material

Materie D -n *f* matter; subject

Matrose D -n, -n *m* sailor; ordinary seaman

Mauer B -n *f* wall

Maus D ⁓e *f* mouse

Mechaniker C -s, - *m* mechanic; engineer

Medizin C -en *f* medicine; science of medicine

Meer A -es, -e *n* sea; ocean; *am Meer* at the seaside; *auf dem Meer* at sea; *übers Meer* oversea(s)

Mehl C -s *n* flour

mehr A *(adj. + adv.)* more; *immer mehr* more and more; *nicht mehr* no more, no longer; *nie mehr* never again; *was noch mehr?* what else?

mehrere A *(adj. pl.)* several

mein A *(poss. adj.)* my; *ich für mein Teil* as far as I'm concerned

meine A -r, -s *(pron.)* mine

meinen A *(w.v.)* think; believe; mean; *wie meinen Sie das?* what do you mean by that?

meinetwegen C *(adv.)* for my part; because of me; *mach' dir meinetwegen keine Sorgen* don't worry about me

Meinung B -en *f* opinion; idea; meaning; *meiner Meinung nach* in my opinion; *derselben Meinung sein* agree [with]

meist[ens] A *(adv.)* mostly; *am meisten* most [of all]; *die meiste Zeit* most of the time

Meister B -s, - *m* master; champion

melden B *(w.v.)* announce; give notice; inform; report; *sich freiwillig melden* volunteer

Melodie B -n *f* melody; tune; air

Menge B -n *f* amount; quantity; a lot; *eine Menge von* a lot of; *in großen Mengen* in great quantities

Mensch A -en, -en *m* human being; man; person; *jeder Mensch* everybody, everyone

Menschheit D *f* mankind; human race; humanity

merken A *(w.v.)* notice, observe; *merken Sie sich meine Worte!* mark my words; *sich merken* retain; remember

merkwürdig B *(adj.)* strange; curious; remarkable

Messe D -n *f* mass (religious); fair

messen B i/a/e measure

Messer B -s, - *n* knife

Metall C -s, -e *n* metal; *aus Metall* metallic

Meter C -s, - *n* metre

Metzger C -s, - *m* butcher

mich A *(pron.)* me

mieten C *(w.v.)* rent; hire; *zu vermieten* to let

Milch B *f* milk

Million B -en *f* million

mindestens C *(adv.)* at least

Minister D -s, - *m* minister; Secretary of State

Minute B -n *f* minute; *auf die Minute kommen* arrive on time

mir A *(pron.)* [to] me; *ich wasche mir die Hände* I wash
my hands

mischen B *(w.v.)* mix; blend

mißlingen D i/a/u fail

mißverstehen D e/a/a misunderstand; mistake

Mist D -es *m* manure; junk; muck

mit A *(prep.)* with; by [means of]; *mit einem Mal* all of
a sudden; *mit der Zeit* in time

mitbringen C i/a/a bring; bring along/with

miteinander D *(adv.)* together; with each other; *alle miteinander* one and all

Mitglied C -s, -er *n* member; fellow

Mitleid C -s *n* pity; compassion; *Mitleid haben* [*mit*]
have pity [on]

mitnehmen B i/a/o take along

Mittag C -s, -e *m* midday; noon; *zu Mittag essen* have
dinner/lunch; *zu Mittag* at noon

mittags D *(adv.)* at noon; at lunch-time

Mitte A -n *f* middle; centre; *in der Mitte* in the middle,
amidst

mitteilen B *(w.v.)* make known; communicate

Mittel A -s, - *n* means; remedy; *er ist ohne Mittel* he is
penniless; *Mittel und Wege* ways and means

Mittelpunkt C -s, -e *m* centre; *Mittelpunkt der Stadt*
heart/centre of the town

mitten [**in**] C *(adv.)* in the middle [of]

Mitternacht D *f* midnight; *um Mitternacht* at midnight

Möbel B -s, - *n* piece of furniture; furniture *(pl.)*

möchte → **mögen**

Mode C -n *f* fashion; style; *aus der Mode kommen* grow
out of fashion

modern B *(adj.)* modern; up-to-date

mögen A a/o/o like; care for; want; may; might; *ich
möchte gern* I should like; *ich möchte wissen* I wonder;
möchten Sie? would you be kind enough [to]?

möglich B *(adj.)* possible; *es ist ihm nicht möglich* it's not possible for him; *so schnell wie möglich* as quickly as possible; *alles mögliche* all sort of things

Möglichkeit C -en *f* possibility; chance

Moment C -s, -e *m* moment; *Moment, bitte!* just a moment, please!

Monat A -s, -e *m* month; *der Monat Januar* the month of January

Mond A -es, -e *m* moon; *der Mond scheint* the moon is shining

Mord C -es, -e *m* murder; *einen Mord begehen* commit a murder

morgen B *(adv.)* tomorrow; *morgen früh* tomorrow morning; *heute morgen* this morning; *bis morgen!* see you tomorrow!

Morgen B -s, - *m* morning; *am Morgen* in the morning; *guten Morgen!* good morning!

morgens C *(adv.)* in the morning; *um 3 Uhr morgens* at 3 o'clock in the morning

Motor B -s, -en *m* motor; engine; *den Motor anlassen/ anwerfen* start the engine; *den Motor abstellen* switch off the engine

Motorrad D -s, ⸚er *n* motor-cycle; motor-bike

Mücke D -n *f* gnat; mosquito

müde A *(adj.)* tired; *müde werden* get tired;

Mühe B -n *f* trouble; pains *(pl.)*; effort; *mit großer Mühe* with great difficulty; *sich die Mühe machen* take the trouble [to]

Mühle D -n *f* mill; windmill

Mund A -es, ⸚er *m* mouth; *den Mund halten* hold one's tongue, shut up; *ein Mundvoll* a mouthful

Mündung D -en *f* mouth, muzzle [of a gun]; estuary

Musik A *f* music; *Musik machen* make music

Muskel C -s, -n *m* muscle

müssen A u/u/u have to; be to; be obliged to; *er muß fort sein* I suppose he's gone; *ich müßte* I ought to

Muster B -s, - *n* model; example; sample

Mut C **-es,** *m* courage; spirit; heart; *den Mut sinken lassen* lose courage; *nur Mut!* cheer up!

Mutter A ⁼ *f* mother

Mütze D **-n** *f* cap; bonnet

N

na! well!; why!; *na also!* then!; *na so was!* dear, dear!

nach A *(prep.)* to; toward(s); after; past; according to; *der Zug nach Berlin* the train for Berlin; *nach dem Essen* after dinner; *nach meiner Uhr* by my watch; *nach Hause* home; *nach und nach* gradually, little by little; bit by bit

Nachbar C **-n, -n** *m* neighbour

nachdem D *(conj.)* after; when

nachdenken [über] C e/a/a think about; reflect [on]

nacheinander C *(adv.)* one after another; in turn

Nachfrage C **-n** *f* inquiry; demand; *Angebot und Nachfrage* supply and demand

nachgehen C e/i/a follow; be slow; lose time; *die Uhr geht 3 Minuten nach* the clock is 3 minutes slow

nachher C *(adv.)* after; afterwards; later

Nachmittag B **-s, -e** *m* afternoon; *heute nachmittag* this afternoon; *am Nachmittag* in the afternoon

nachmittags D *(adv.)* in the afternoon

Nachricht B **-en** *f* news *(pl.)*; intelligence; *letzte Nachrichten* last/last-minute news

nachsehen C ie/a/e check; look after

nächst C *(adj. sup.)* next; *nächsten Montag* next Monday; *nächster Tage* one of these days

Nacht B ⁼e *f* night; *bei Nacht* by night; *eines Nachts* one night; *gute Nacht!* good-night!; *es wird Nacht* it's growing/getting dark

nachts D *(adv.)* at night; by night; *bis 2 Uhr nachts* till two in the morning

nackt D *(adj.)* naked; nude; bare
Nadel B **-n** *f* pin; needle; *ich sitze wie auf Nadeln* I'm on pins and needles
Nagel B **-s,** ⁔ *m* nail
nahe [bei] A *(adj.)* near; close by; *von nah und fern* from far and near
nahezu D *(adv.)* nearly
Nähe C *f* vicinity; neighbourhood; *in der Nähe* not far off; *aus der Nähe* from nearby
nähen B *(w.v.)* sew; stitch; *einen Knopf annähen* sew on a button
nahm → **nehmen**
Nahrung D *f* food; nourishment
Name A **-n(s), -n** *m* name; *im Namen* on behalf of
namentlich D *(adv.)* particularly; especially
nämlich B *(adv.)* namely; that is to say
Narr D **-en, -en** *m* fool; jester; *sei kein Narr!* don't be a fool!
Nase A **-n** *f* nose; *sich die Nase putzen* blow one's nose
naß C *(adj.)* wet; *naß werden* get wet/soaked
Nation C **-en** *f* nation; *die vereinten Nationen* the United Nations
Natur B **-en** *f* nature; *von Natur aus* by nature
natürlich A *(adj.)* natural; naturally; of course
Nebel C **-s, -** *m* mist; fog
neben A *(prep.)* beside; by the side of; close by; besides
nebenan C *(adv.)* next door; close by
nebenbei D *(adv.)* by the way; besides
nebeneinander C *(adv.)* side by side
nehmen A **i/a/o** take; *den Bus nehmen* take the bus; *wie man's nimmt!* that depends! *Platz nehmen* have a seat
Neid D **-s** *m* envy; jealousy; *aus Neid* out of envy
neigen D *(w.v.)* bend; incline
nein A *(adv.)* no; *nein sagen* deny
nennen A **e/a/a** name; call; mention; *sich nennen* be called

Nerv C **-s, -en** *m* nerve; *auf die Nerven gehen* get on one's nerves

nett B *(adj.)* nice; pretty

Netz D **-es, -e** *n* net; network

neu A *(adj.)* new; recent; *aufs neue* anew; *wieder neu anfangen* start all over again

Neugier C *f* curiosity

Neuheit C **-en** *f* novelty

Neuigkeit D **-en** *f* [a piece of] news

neulich B *(adv.)* recently; the other day

nicht A *(adv.)* not; *noch nicht* not yet; *auch nicht* not either; *nicht einmal* not even

nicht nur . . . sondern auch B not only . . . but also

nichts A *(pron.)* nothing; not anything; *gar nichts* nothing at all; *nichts mehr* no more

nie A *(adv.)* never; *fast nie* hardly ever; *nie wieder* never again

nieder D *(adv.)* down; *auf und nieder* up and down

niedrig A *(adj.)* low; mean; inferior

niemals B *(adv.)* never; *fast niemals* hardly ever

niemand A *(pron.)* nobody; no one; *niemand anders* nobody else

nimmt → **nehmen**

nirgends A *(adv.)* nowhere; not anywhere

noch A *(adv.)* still; more; yet; *noch einmal* once more; *noch nicht* not yet; *noch immer* still; *noch etwas* something else; *noch heute* this very day

Norden B **-s** *m* north; *gegen Norden* to the north

normal C *(adj.)* normal; regular

Not C ⁓e *f* want; need; danger; *Not leiden* suffer want; *in Not sein* be in trouble

nötig B *(adj.)* necessary; *nötig haben* need, want

notwendig B *(adj.)* necessary

Null B **-en** *f* zero; nil

Nummer C **-n** *f* number; size; *eine Nummer wählen* dial a number

nun A *(adv.)* now; at present; *nun!* well!; *von nun an* from
now on; *was nun?* what next?

nur A *(adv.)* only; just; *wenn nur* provided that, if only;
nicht nur . . . sondern auch not only . . . but also

Nutzen D -s *m* use; profit; *von Nutzen sein* be of service

nützen C *(w.v.)* be useful; *es nützt nicht* it's no use

nützlich D *(adj.)* useful

O

ob A *(conj.)* whether; *als ob* as if; *nicht als ob* not that

oben A *(adv.)* above; up; on top; *dort oben* up there;
nach oben upwards, upstairs; *von oben bis unten* from
top to bottom

ober C *(adj.)* upper; superior

Oberfläche D -n *f* surface

Obst C -es *n* fruit; *Obstbaum* fruit-tree

Ochse D -n, -n *m* ox

oder A *(conj.)* or

Ofen C -s, ⁓ *m* stove; oven; furnace

offen A *(adj.)* open; frank; *offen gesagt* to be honest

öffentlich C *(adj.)* public; *öffentliche Meinung* public
opinion

öffnen A *(w.v.)* open; unlock

oft A *(adv.)* often; *so oft wie möglich* as often as possible

ohne A *(prep.)* without

Ohr A -s, -en *n* ear

Öl A -s, -e *n* oil

Omnibus B -ses, -se *m* bus; motor coach

Onkel C -s, - *m* uncle

Operation D -en *f* operation

Opfer D -s, - *n* sacrifice; victim; *ein Opfer bringen* make
a sacrifice

ordnen C *(w.v.)* put in order; tidy; arrange

Ordnung B **-en** ƒ order; arrangement; [*alles*] *in Ordnung!*
all right!

Ort A **-es,⁓er** *m* place; spot

Osten B **-s** *m* east; *im Osten* in the east

Ostern D *(pl.)* Easter; *zu Ostern* at Easter; *Fröhliche
Ostern!* Happy Easter!

Ozean D **-s, -e** *m* ocean; *der Stille Ozean* the Pacific

P

Paar B **-s, -e** *n* pair; couple; *ein Paar Schuhe* a pair of
shoes

ein paar B a few; *vor ein paar Tagen* a few days ago, the
other day

packen B *(w.v.)* pack, seize; *den Koffer packen* pack one's
trunk/suit-case; *er packte ihn am Arm* he seized him
by the arm; *pack dich!* get out of here!

Panne D **-n** ƒ breakdown; *eine Panne haben* have a breakdown

Papier A **-s, -e** *n* paper; *ein Bogen/Blatt Papier* a sheet of
paper; *zu Papier bringen* write down

Park D **-s, -s** *m* park

parken C *(w.v.)* park; *parken verboten!* no parking!

Partei D **-en** ƒ party; *Partei nehmen für* take sides with

Paß C **-sses,⁓sse** *m* pass; passport

passen B *(w.v.)* fit; suit; *das paßt sich nicht* that's not
done; *das paßt mir gut* that suits me well

passieren C *(w.v.)* pass; cross; occur; happen

Patient D **-en, -en** *m* patient

Pause C **-n** ƒ pause; break; interval

Person A **-en** ƒ person; character

persönlich C *(adj.)* personal

Pfeife B **-n** ƒ whistle; pipe; *Pfeife rauchen* smoke one's
pipe

pfeifen D **ei/i/i** whistle
Pfennig C **-s, -e** *m* penny
Pferd A **-es, -e** *n* horse; *zu Pferde* on horseback
Pflanze B **-n** *f* plant
pflanzen D *(w.v.)* plant; set; lay out
pflegen B *(w.v.)* take care of; care for; nurse
Pflicht D **-en** *f* duty
pflücken D *(w.v.)* pick; pluck; gather
Pflug D **-s, ⁼e** *m* plough
Pfund B **-s, -e** *n* pound; *2 Pfund Obst* 2 pounds of fruit
Phantasie D **-n** *f* imagination
Pinsel C **-s, -** *m* brush; paint-brush
Plan C **-s, ⁼e** *m* plan; scheme; map; *einen Plan durch-führen/ausführen* carry out a plan
Platz A **-es, ⁼e** *m* place; space; *Platz nehmen* take a seat; *Platz machen* make room [for]; *Plätze bestellen* book seats
platzen B *(w.v.)* burst; split; crack
plötzlich A *(adj.)* suddenly; all of a sudden
Politik C *f* politics
politisch C *(adj.)* political
Polizei C *f* police; *die Polizei rufen* call the police
Polizist D **-en, -en** *m* policeman; constable
Post A *f* post; mail; post-office; *die Post erledigen* answer the mail; *zur Post bringen* post/mail; *mit der Post* by mail
Posten C **-s, -** *m* post; situation, job; sentry
praktisch C *(adj.)* practical
Präsident D **-en, -en** *m* president; chairman
Preis A **-es, -e** *m* 1. price; *um keinen Preis* not at any price; *zum Preise von* at the price of. 2. prize; *einen Preis gewinnen* win a prize
Presse D *f* press
prima C *(adj.)* first rate; *prima!* wonderful!
privat D *(adj.)* private
Problem D **-s, -e** *n* problem; *ein Problem lösen* solve a problem

Produkt D -s, -e *n* product

Programm D -s, -e *n* program(me); schedule

Prozent C -s, -e *n* per cent

prüfen B *(w.v.)* examine; test; try

Prüfung C -en *f* examination; testing; *eine Prüfung be-stehen* pass an examination

Publikum C -s *n* public

Pult D -s, -e *n* desk

Punkt C -s, -e *m* point; full stop; period; *in diesem Punkt* in this respect; *nach Punkten verlieren* lose on points; *Punkt 3 Uhr* at 3 o'clock sharp

pünktlich D *(adj.)* punctual; on time; *pünktlich sein* be on time

putzen C *(w.v.)* clean; cleanse; *sich die Nase putzen* blow one's nose

Q

Qualität D -en *f* quality; *erster Qualität* first-rate; *schlechte Qualität* poor quality

Quantität D -en *f* quantity; amount

Quelle B -n *f* spring; source; well; *aus erster Quelle* first-hand (information); *die Stromquelle* source of power

quer C *(adv.)* across; *kreuz und quer* all over, this way and that

R

Rad A -es, ⁀er *n* wheel; bicycle; *radfahren* ride a bicycle

Radio A -s, -s *n* radio; wireless; radio(set); *im Radio sprechen* speak over the radio; *Radio hören* listen to the radio

Rakete D -n *f* rocket; *eine Rakete abfeuern* launch/shoot a rocket

rasch A *(adj.)* quick; *machen Sie rasch!* be quick!, hurry up!

rasieren C *(w.v.)* shave; *sich rasieren lassen* get shaved

Rat B **-s** *m* 1. advice; *um Rat fragen* ask advice; *mit Rat und Tat* by word and deed. 2. council; board; *Rathaus* town-hall

raten B **ä/ie/a** 1. advice; give advice. 2. guess; *raten Sie mal!* give a guess!

Rauch D **-s** *m* smoke; *in Rauch aufgehen* come to nóthing

rauchen C *(w.v.)* smoke; *Rauchen verboten!* No smoking!; *Pfeife rauchen* smoke one's pipe

Raum A **-s, ⸚e** *m* room; space; *die Räume des Hauses* the rooms of the house; *Raumflug* space-flight

rechnen A *(w.v.)* reckon; calculate; *dazu rechnen* add

Rechnung B **-en** *f* bill; account; invoice; *die Rechnung bitte!* the bill please!

Recht C **-s, -e** *n* right; justice; *die Rechte studieren* study law; *das Recht haben* have the right; *ohne Recht* unjustly

recht A *(adj.)* right; fair; well; *du hast recht* you are right; *du hast nicht recht* you are wrong; *zur rechten Zeit* in due time; *recht geben* agree; *ganz recht!* just so!, quite!

rechts B *(adv.)* right; on the right; *nach rechts* to the right; *zweite Straße rechts* second turn to the right

Rede B **-n** *f* talk; speech; *eine Rede halten [über]* make/ deliver a speech [on]; *nicht der Rede wert* not worth mentioning

reden B *(w.v.)* talk; speak; *mit dir reden* talk to you; *über etwas reden* talk about something

Regel C **-n** *f* rule; principle; *in der Regel* as a rule; generally

regeln D *(w.v.)* regulate; control

sich regen D *(w.v.)* stir; be active

Regen A **-s, -** *m* rain; *starker Regen* heavy rain; *es regnet* it is raining

Regierung C **-en** *f* government

reiben D **ei/ie/ie** rub; *sich die Hände reiben* rub one's hands; *ich rieb es ihr unter die Nase* I drummed it into her; *gerieben* cunning, sly

reich B *(adj.)* rich; well off; *eine reiche Auswahl* a wide selection

reichen B *(w.v.)* hand; pass; present; *das reicht!* that will do!; *reichen Sie mir bitte . . .* would you pass me . .

reif C *(adj.)* ripe; mature; *reif werden* ripen

Reifen C -s, - *m* tyre; US: tire; *Reifen wechseln* change tyres/tires

Reihe A -n *f* file; range, row; set; series; line; *in einer Reihe* in a row/line; *außer der Reihe* out of turn;

rein A *(adj.)* pure; clean; tidy; *die reine Wahrheit* the plain truth; *reiner Unsinn* sheer nonsense

Reise B -n *f* journey; travel; voyage; trip; *Glückliche/ Gute Reise!* have a nice trip!

reisen B *(w.v.)* travel; *von Hamburg nach Berlin reisen* go from Hamburg to Berlin; *mit der Eisenbahn reisen* go by rail/train

reißen B ei/i/i tear; tear off; break; *in Stücke reißen* tear to pieces; *der Faden reißt* the thread breaks

reiten B ei/i/i ride; go on horseback

Religion A -en *f* religion

rennen B e/a/a run; rush

Reparatur D -en *f* repair; mending; *in Reparatur* under repair; *reparieren* repair

Republik C -en *f* republic

Rest B -es, -e *m* rest; remains *(pl.)*

Restaurant C -s, -s *n* restaurant; tavern

retten C *(w.v.)* save; rescue

Revolution A -en *f* revolution

richten D *(w.v.)* 1. direct; *sich richten nach* act according to. 2. judge; *sich richten [an]* address oneself [to]; *zu Grunde richten* ruin

Richter D -s, - *m* judge; *vor den Richter bringen* bring to justice

richtig A *(adj.)* right; correct; exact; *richtig!* quite right!; *die Uhr geht richtig* the watch is right

Richtung A -en *f* direction; way; *in gerader Richtung* straight on; *die Richtung verlieren* lose one's way

riechen A ie/o/o smell; scent; stink; *riechen nach* smell of; *riechen an* smell at; *das konnte ich doch nicht riechen?* how could I know?

rief → **rufen**

Rind D -s, -er *n* ox; cow; cattle

Ring A -s, -e *m* ring; circle

rings D *(adv.)* (a)round

Rock A -s,⸚e *m* coat; jacket; skirt

roh C *(adj.)* raw; crude; rough; coarse; *roher Mensch* brute; *rohes Fleisch* raw meat/flesh

Rolle B -n *f* roll; roller; part; role; *eine Rolle spielen* play a part; *das spielt keine Rolle* that doesn't matter

Roman D -s, -e *m* novel

Rose B -n *f* rose

rot A *(adj.)* red; *rot werden* turn red, blush; *das Rote Kreuz* the Red Cross

Rücken C -s, - *m* back; *im Rücken* in the rear

Rückkehr D *f* return; returning

rückwärts D *(adv.)* backward(s); *rückwärts fahren* back [up], reverse

Ruf C -s, -e *m* call; cry; yell; *in gutem Ruf stehen* have a good reputation; *Rufnummer* (tele)phone number

rufen A u/ie/u call; cry; shout; *wie gerufen kommen* come at the right moment; *die Polizei rufen* call for the police

Ruhe A *f* quiet; calm; rest; *Ruhe!* silence!; *in Ruhe lassen* let alone; *zur Ruhe bringen* calm down; *immer mit der Ruhe!* take it easy!

ruhen C *(w.v.)* rest; sleep; cease working

ruhig A *(adj.)* calm; silent; quiet; *sei ruhig!* keep quiet! *ruhig schlafen* sleep soundly

rühren D *(w.v.)* stir; move; touch; *das rührt mich nicht* that makes no impression on me; *rührt euch!* stand at ease!

rund A *(adj.)* round

Rundfunk B -s *m* radio; wireless; *im Rundfunk* on the radio

runter = **herunter**

S

Sache A -n *f* thing; affair; matter; *das ist meine Sache* that's my business; *die ganze Sache* the whole thing; *die vorliegende Sache* the subject in hand; *bei der Sache bleiben* stick to the point

Sack D -s, ⸚e *m* sack; bag; *die Katze im Sack kaufen* buy a pig in a poke

säen D *(w.v)* sow

Saft C -s, ⸚e *m* juice

sagen A *(w.v.)* say; tell; *sagen wir ...* suppose ...; *man sagt* they/people say; *es hat nichts zu sagen* it doesn't matter; *wie gesagt* as I said before; *wie sagt man ... auf Deutsch?* what is the German for ...?, how do you say ... in German?

sah → **sehen**

Salz B -es, -e *n* salt

sammeln C *(w.v.)* gather; collect; *Briefmarken sammeln* collect stamps

sämtliche D *(adj. pl.)* all; *sämtliche Werke* complete works

Sand D -s, -e *m* sand; *im Sand verlaufen* come to nothing

sanft D *(adj.)* soft; tender; gentle; *ruhe sanft!* rest in peace!

saß → **sitzen**

satt B *(adj.)* satisfied; full; *ich bin satt* I've had enough; *ich habe es satt* I'm sick of it, I'm fed up with it

Satz C -es, ⸚e 1. leap; bound. 2. sentence; phrase. 3. set

sauber B *(adj.)* clean; neat; tidy; *sauber machen* clean [up]

sauer C *(adj.)* sour; acid; *die Milch ist sauer geworden* the milk has turned [sour]

Schachtel D -n *f* box; case

schade C *(adv.)* : *es ist schade* it's a pity; *wie schade!* what a pity!

schaden C *(w.v.)* damage; [do] harm; hurt; *das schadet nichts* that doesn't matter; *sich selbst schaden* discredit oneself

Schaden C -s, ⁀ *m* damage; harm; *Schaden leiden* suffer damages; *niemand kam zu Schaden* no one was hurt

Schaf D -s, -e *n* sheep

schaffen B a/u/a create; produce; *eine Rolle schaffen* create a role

schälen D *(w.v.)* peel; skin

Schallplatte D -n *f* record; *eine Schallplatte auflegen* put on a record

schalten D *(w.v.)* change; switch

Schalter C -s, - *m* switch; booking office; counter; *gehen Sie zum Schalter!* go to the counter!

scharf B *(adj.)* sharp; keen; *scharf betonen* accent strongly

Schatten B -s, - *m* shade; shadow; *im Schatten sitzen* sit in the shade

schätzen D *(w.v.)* estimate; value; respect; *sich glücklich schätzen* be happy [to]

Schauspiel D -s, -e *n* play; drama; spectacle

Scheck D -s, -s *m* cheque; US: check; *einen Scheck ausstellen* draw a cheque/check

Schein A -s, -e *m* 1. shine; light. 2. note; bill. 3. appearance; *den Schein geben, als ob* pretend to

scheinen A ei/ie/ie shine; seem; appear; *es scheint mir* it appears to me; *wie es scheint* as it seems

Scheinwerfer D -s, - *m* head-light; search-light; flood-light

schenken C *(w.v.)* 1. give; present. 2. pour out

Schere C -n *f* [a pair of] scissors

schicken A *(w.v.)* send; post; mail; *mit der Post schicken* post/mail; *nach dem Arzt schicken* send for the doctor

Schicksal D -s, -e *n* destiny; fortune; fate; *sein Schicksal ist besiegelt* his fate is sealed

schieben D ie/o/o push; shove; *in die Tasche schieben* put into one's pocket

schief B *(adj.)* sloping; slant(ing); *in einer schiefen Lage sein* be in an awkward position; *es geht schief* things are going wrong

schien → **scheinen**

schießen B ie/o/o shoot; *tot schießen* kill; *ein Tor schießen* score a goal

Schiff A -s, -e *n* ship; vessel; boat; *auf dem Schiff* on board; *das Schiff verlassen* abandon ship

Schirm D -s, -e *m* screen; umbrella

Schlaf B -s *m* sleep; *im Schlaf* in one's sleep; *ohne Schlaf* sleepless

schlafen A ä/ie/a sleep; be asleep; *schlafen Sie wohl!* sleep well!; *über etwas schlafen* sleep on something; *schlafen gehen* go to bed

Schlag A -s, ⸚e *m* blow; knock; *mit einem Schlag* at one blow/stroke

schlagen A ä/u/a beat; strike; knock; hit; *das Herz schlägt dir* your heart beats; *es schlägt 3 [Uhr]* it's just striking three

schlecht A *(adj.)* bad; *schlechtes Wetter* nasty weather; *schlechte Zeiten* hard times; *mir ist schlecht* I feel ill/sick

schließen A ie/o/o shut; close; lock; *die Augen schließen* close/shut one's eyes; *in die Arme schließen* embrace

schließlich C *(adv.)* finally; after all; *schließlich und endlich* when all is said and done

schlimm A *(adj.)* bad; evil; *eine schlimme Geschichte* a sad tale; *es sieht schlimm aus* it looks bad

Schloß C -sses, ⸚sser *n* 1. castle; palace. 2. lock; padlock

Schluck D -s, -e *m* mouthful; sip; *einen Schluck nehmen* have a sip

schlucken D *(w.v.)* swallow; gulp

Schluß A -sses, ⸚sse *m* end; close; *am Schluß* at the end;

zum Schluß in the end; *Schluß machen* finish; *Schluß damit!* stop it!

Schlüssel C **-s, -** *m* key;

schmal B *(adj.)* narrow; slender; thin

schmecken B *(w.v.)* taste; try; *es schmeckt mir nicht* I don't like it; *gut schmecken* taste good; *wie schmeckt's?* how do you like it?

Schmerz B **-es, -en** *m* pain; ache; *ich habe Schmerzen* I feel pains; *heftige Schmerzen* severe pains

schmutzig B *(adj.)* dirty; soiled; *schmutzig machen* soil, dirty

Schnee D **-s** *m* snow

schneiden A **ei/i/i** cut; mow; carve; *in Stücke schneiden* cut to pieces; *sich die Haare schneiden lassen* have one's hair cut

Schneider D **-s, -** *m* tailor; dressmaker

schnell A *(adj.)* fast; quick; rapid, swift; *schnell wie der Blitz* as quick as lightning; *immer schneller* faster and faster; *mach schnell!* hurry up!

Schnupfen D **-s** *m* cold; *den Schnupfen haben* have a cold

Schnur C **-en** *f* cord; string; line

Schokolade B **-n** *f* chocolate; *eine Tafel Schokolade* a bar of chocolate

schon A *(adv.)* already; *es ist schon 2 Uhr* it's already two o'clock; *ist er schon gekommen?* has he come yet?; *schon heute* this very day; *ich verstehe schon* Oh, I see; *es wird schon gehen* surely it will turn out all right

schön A *(adj.)* beautiful; handsome; nice; fine; *schönen Dank!* thanks!; *wie schön!* how nice!; *eines schönen Tages* one fine day; *schönes Wetter* fine weather

Schönheit C **-en** *f* beauty

Schrank C **-es, ⸚e** *m* wardrobe; locker; cupboard

Schreck[en] B **-s** *m* terror; fright; fear; horror; *vor Schreck(en) bleich werden* turn pale with fear

schreiben A **ei/ie/ie** write; spell; *falsch schreiben* misspell; *mit der Schreibmaschine schreiben* type

schreien A ei/ie/ie cry; shout; *um Hilfe schreien* call [out]
for help

schreiten D ei/i/i walk; step

Schrift C -en *f* writing; *Kopf oder Schrift?* heads or tails?

schriftlich C *(adj.)* written; in writing

Schritt C -s, -e *m* step; *was ist der nächste Schritt?* what
is the next step?

Schuh A -s, -e *m* shoe; boot; *die Schuhe putzen* polish
one's shoes

Schuld D -en *f* debt; fault; *es ist meine Schuld* it's my
fault; *wer ist daran schuld?* who is to blame for it?

schulden D *(w.v.)* owe

schuldig C *(adj.)* guilty; indebted; *was bin ich Ihnen schuldig?* how much do I owe you?

Schule A -n *f* school; *in der Schule* at school; *eine Schule
besuchen* go to a school

Schüler B -s, - *m* pupil; schoolboy

Schülerin B -nen *f* pupil; schoolgirl

Schulter D -n *f* shoulder

Schuß D -sses, ⸚sses *m* shot; round; *einen Schuß abgeben* fire a shot; *in Schuß kommen* rush along

Schüssel C -n *f* dish; bowl; *eine Schüssel Milch* a bowl
of milk

schütteln D *(w.v.)* shake; *sich schütteln* tremble, shiver;
die Hand schütteln shake hands [with]

Schutz C -es *m* protection; defence; *Schutz vor Regen
suchen* take shelter from the rain

schützen C *(w.v.)* protect; defend; *sich schützen gegen*
protect oneself from, guard oneself against

schwach A *(adj.)* weak; feeble; *mir wird schwach* I feel
faint

Schwamm D -s, ⸚e *m* sponge; mushroom; *Schwamm
darüber!* skip it!

Schwanz D -es, ⸚e *m* tail; *der Hund wedelt mit dem
Schwanz* the dog wags its tail

schwarz A *(adj.)* black

schweigen C ei/ie/ie be/keep silent; *ganz zu schweigen von* to say nothing of

Schwein C -es, -e *n* pig; *Schwein haben* be lucky

schwer A *(adj.)* heavy; difficult; grave; serious; *schwer arbeiten* work hard; *schwer atmen* breathe heavily; *es fällt mir sehr schwer* I find it very difficult/hard

Schwester A -n *f* sister; nurse

schwierig B *(adj.)* difficult; hard

Schwierigkeit C -en difficulty; *auf Schwierigkeiten stoßen* encounter difficulties

schwimmen B i/a/o swim; *sie schwimmt in Geld* she's rolling in money

schwitzen C *(w.v.)* perspire; sweat

See C -s, -n *m* lake

See B *f* sea; *auf See* at sea; *zur See gehen* go to sea; *seekrank* sea-sick

Seele D -n *f* soul; mind; spirit; *aus voller Seele* with all one's heart

Segel D -s, - *n* sail

sehen A ie/a/e see; look; *ähnlich sehen* resemble; *sieh mich an* look at me; *laß mal sehen!* let's see!; *schlecht sehen* have bad eyes/eyesight

sehr A *(adv.)* very; much; *sehr gut* very good/well; *sehr gern* most willingly; *zu sehr* too much; *das gefällt mir sehr* I like that very much

Seife C *f* soap; *ein Stück Seife* a cake/bar of soap

sein A [bin; war; bin gewesen] be; exist; *ihm ist übel* he feels sick; *was ist Ihnen?* what's the matter with you? *es ist mir, als wenn* I feel as if; *es sei!* let it be so!

sein A *(poss. adj.)* his; its

seine A [-r, -s] *(pron.)* his; its

seinetwegen D *(adv.)* because of him; for his sake; *sie hat es seinetwegen getan* she did it because of him

seit A *(prep.)* since; for; *seit einiger Zeit* for some time past; *seit wann?* since when?, for how long?; *seit langem* for a long time

seitdem B *(adv.)* since; ever since

Seite A **-n** *f* side; page; *hintere Seite* back; *an die Seite stellen* compare; *nach allen Seiten* in all directions; *es steht auf Seite 10* it says on page 10

Sekunde B **-n** *f* second

selbst A *(pron.)* self; even; *ich selbst* I myself; *selbst kommen* come personally; *selbst seine Eltern* even his parents

selbstverständlich B *(adj.)* of course; *es ist selbstverständlich* that goes without saying

selten B *(adj.)* rare; unusual; *höchst selten* hardly ever; *nicht selten* pretty often

senden B e/a/a send; broadcast; *nachsenden* forward

Sessel D **-s, -** *m* arm-chair; easy-chair

setzen A *(w.v.)* set; place; put; *sich setzen* sit down; *instand setzen* repair

sich A *(pron.)* himself; herself; itself; themselves; yourself; yourselves; oneself; one another; each other; *außer sich sein* be beside oneself; *das spricht für sich selbst* that speaks for itself; *sie lieben sich* they love each other

sicher A *(adj.)* safe; secure; sure; certain; *eine sichere Hand* a steady hand; *sicher!* certainly!

Sicherheit B **-en** *f* safety; security; *in Sicherheit bringen* put in a safe place

sichtbar D *(adj.)* visible

sie A *(pron.)* she; her; they; them

Sie A *(pron.)* you

Sieg D **-es, -e** *m* victory; conquest

siegen D *(w.v.)* win; conquer

sieht → **sehen**

Silber B **-s** *n* silver; *aus Silber* [made] of silver

sind → **sein**

singen A i/a/u sing

sinken B i/a/u sink; go down; *den Mut sinken lassen* lose courage; *die Preise sinken* prices are going down

Sinn B -es, -e *m* sense; mind; meaning; *die fünf Sinne*
the five senses; *sich etwas aus dem Sinn schlagen* put
something out of one's mind; *das hat keinen Sinn* that
doesn't make sense; *Sinn haben für* have a feeling for

Sitz B -es, -e *m* seat; chair

sitzen A i/a/e sit; be seated; *bei Tisch sitzen* sit at table;
dieser Anzug sitzt gut this suit fits well

Sitzung D -en *f* session; meeting

so A *(adv.)* so; thus; such; in that manner; *Ach so!* Oh,
I see! *so daß* so that; *so . . . wie* as . . . as; *so oder so*
this way or that way

sobald C *(conj.)* as soon as

Socke C -n *f* sock

so daß A *(conj.)* so that; so as to

soeben B *(adv.)* just; this minute

Sofa C -s, -s *n* sofa; couch

sofort A *(adv.)* immediately; at once; right away; *sofort!*
coming!

sogar B *(adv.)* even

sogenannt D *(adj.)* so-called; would-be

Sohn A -es, ⸚e *m* son

solange C *(adv.)* as long as; while

solche [-r, -s] B *(adj.)* such; *ein solcher Mann* such a man;
solch ein Mann such a man; *solche Leute (pl.)* such
people *(pl.)*

Soldat A -en, -en *m* soldier; *gemeiner Soldat* private;
alter Soldat veteran

sollen A o/o/o shall; should; ought; be to; have to; *ich
soll morgen fahren* I am to go tomorrow; *ich soll die
Rechnung morgen bezahlen* I have to pay the bill tomorrow; *man sollte meinen* one should think; *ich sollte
eigentlich schreiben* I ought to write

Sommer B -s, - *m* summer; *im Sommer* in [the] summer,
during [the] summer; *der Sommer ist vorbei* the summer is over

sonderbar C *(adj.)* strange; singular; *mir ist so sonderbar*
I am/feel very queer

sondern A *(conj.)* but; *nicht nur . . . sondern auch* not only . . . but also

Sonne A **-n** *f* sun; *in der Sonne liegen* lie in the sun; *die Sonne scheint* the sun shines; *die Sonne geht auf* the sun is rising; *die Sonne geht unter* the sun is setting

sonst C *(adv.)* otherwise; else; *sonst nichts* nothing else

Sorge C **-n** *f* sorrow; care; trouble; worry; *sich Sorge machen* [*um*] be worried [about]

sorgen C *(w.v.)* take care; attend to; see to; *ich sorge dafür* I'll see to it

sorgfältig D *(adj.)* careful; accurate

soweit C *(conj.)* as far as; as much as

sowie D *(conj.)* as well as; as soon as

sowieso C *(adv.)* anyway; in any case

Sowjetunion A *f* the Soviet Union, the U.S.S.R.

sowohl . . . als [auch] C as well . . . as; both . . . and

sozial C *(adj.)* social; public

sozusagen D *(adv.)* so to speak; as it were

spalten C *(w.v.)* split; crack; divide; *Haare spalten* split hairs

spannen C *(w.v.)* stretch; tighten; stress; *gespannt sein* be curious

sparen C *(w.v.)* save [up]; spare; put by; *seine Worte sparen* spare one's words

Spaß B **-es, ⸚e** *m* joke; fun; amusement; *zum Spaß* for fun; *nur zum Spaß* just for the fun of it; *schlechter Spaß* bad joke; *viel Spaß!* enjoy yourself!, have a good time!; *es macht mir Spaß* it amuses me, I like it; *Spaß beiseite!* joking aside!

spät A *(adj.)* late; *spät kommen* be late; *wie spät ist es?* what time is it?; *es wird schon spät* it is getting late; *spät am Tage* late in the day

spazierenfahren B **ä/u/a** go for a drive; take a drive; *spazierengehen* go for a walk

Speise D **-n** *f* food; meal; dish; *Speisekarte* menu; *Speisekammer* larder

Spiegel C **-s, -** *m* mirror; (looking-)glass

Spiel A -s, -e *n* play; game; sport; match; *aufs Spiel setzen* stake, risk;

spielen A *(w.v.)* play; *ein Spiel spielen* play [at] a game; *eine Rolle spielen* play/act a part; *Karten spielen* play [at] cards; *ein Instrument spielen* play an instrument; *das spielt keine Rolle* that doesn't matter

spitz B *(adj.)* pointed; sharp

Spitze C -n *f* point; top; summit; peak; head; *an der Spitze* in the lead, ahead

Sport B -es *m* sport; athletics *(pl.)*; *Sport treiben* go in for sport

sprach → **sprechen**

Sprache B -n *f* language; speech; tongue; *heraus mit der Sprache!* speak out/up!; *fremde Sprachen* foreign languages

sprechen A i/a/o speak; talk; *Englisch sprechen* speak English; *groß sprechen* brag; *er ist nicht zu sprechen* he is not available, he's not in; *hier spricht X* this is X speaking

springen A i/a/u jump; spring; hop; run; *auf die Füße springen* jump/leap to one's feet; *vor Freude springen* leap for joy

Staat C -es, -en *m* state; *in vollem Staat* in full dress

Stab B -es, ⁔e *m* staff; stick; *am Stabe gehen* walk with the help of a stick

Stadt A⁔e *f* town; city; *in der Stadt sein* be in town

Stahl D -s *m* steel; *aus Stahl* [made] of steel

Stall D -s, ⁔e *m* stable; cowshed

Stamm D -es, ⁔e *m* trunk; stem; breed; stock; *der Apfel fällt nicht weit vom Stamm* like father, like son

stand → **stehen**

Stand C -es, ⁔e *m* standing; position; profession; *gut im Stand* in good condition; *zustande bringen* bring about, accomplish

Standpunkt D -s, -e *m* point of view; standpoint

stark A *(adj.)* strong; powerful; great; *eine starke Stunde* a full hour; *das ist ein starkes Stück* that is too bad

Stärke B **-n** *f* strength; force; power; energy; *meine Stärke* my strong point

Start C **-s, -e** *m* start; take-off; *Start und Ziel* start and finish

starten C *(w.v.)* start

statt A *(prep.)* instead of; *statt meiner* in my place

stattfinden D **i/a/u** take place; happen

Staub C **-es** *m* dust; powder; *Staub wischen* dust; *in den Staub ziehen* degrade

staunen C *(w.v.)* be astonished; wonder; be amazed

stechen D **i/a/o** prick; sting; bite; stab

stecken C *(w.v.)* stick; put; place; *in die Tasche stecken* put in one's pocket; *wo steckst du?* where are you?

stehen A **e/a/a** stand; become, suit; *es steht bei ihm* it rests with him; *die Uhr steht* the watch has stopped; *wie steht's?* how are you?; *das steht Ihnen gut* that suits you

stehlen D **ie/a/o** steal; *sich in das Zimmer stehlen* steal into the room

steigen A **ei/ie/ie** climb; rise; mount; ascend; board, enter; *aus dem Bett steigen* get out of bed; *zu Pferd steigen* mount a horse; *die Aktien steigen* the shares rise; *an Land steigen* go ashore

Stein B **-s, -e** *m* stone; rock; *aus Stein* [made] of stone

Stelle A **-n** *f* place; spot; point; post; job; *auf der Stelle* at once, straight away, then and there; *ohne Stelle sein* be unemployed; *an erster Stelle* in the first place; *an meiner Stelle* in my place

stellen A *(w.v.)* put; set; place; provide; adjust; *eine Falle stellen* set a trap; *eine Frage stellen* ask a question; *auf den Kopf stellen* turn upside down

Stellung C **-en** *f* position; situation; job

sterben C **i/a/o** die; pass away; *Hungers sterben* die of hunger

Stern B **-s, -e** *m* star

stets C *(adv.)* always; constantly

still A *(adj.)* still; motionless; calm; silent; *still!* silence!;
der stille Ozean the Pacific

Stille D *f* silence; peace; *in aller Stille* secretly, privately

Stimme B -n *f* voice; vote; *seine Stimme abgeben* vote,
cast one's vote; *mit lauter Stimme* in a loud voice

stimmen C *(w.v.)* tune; put in tune; vote; *das Instrument
stimmen* tune the instrument; *dafür oder dagegen
stimmen* vote for or against; *das stimmt!* that's correct!, that's true enough!

Stimmung C -en *f* mood; temper; humour; *in guter
Stimmung sein* be in a good humour/mood

Stock B -s, ⁻e *m* 1. stick; rod; cane. 2. floor *im ersten
Stock* on the first floor

Stoff C -s, -e *m* substance; matter; material; fabric;
cloth

stolz C *(adj.)* proud; *stolz sein auf* be proud of

stören B *(w.v.)* disturb; trouble; bother; *den Frieden stören* break the peace; *stören Sie mich nicht!* don't bother
me! *Bitte nicht stören!* Please, don't disturb

stoßen B ö/ie/o push; shove, knock

Strafe C -n *f* punishment; fine; penalty; *eine Strafe
zahlen* pay a fine

Strahl D -s, -en *m* ray; beam; jet

Straße A -n *f* street; road; *an der Straße* by the roadside;
auf der Straße in the street; *über die Straße gehen* cross
the street

streben D *(w.v.)* strive; aim at

Strecke C -n *f* stretch; distance; *eine Strecke zurück-
legen* cover a distance

streichen B ei/i/i stroke; pass [over]; touch gently; paint;
glatt streichen smooth; polish; *frisch gestrichen!* wet
paint!

Streichholz C -es, ⁻er *n* match; *ein Streichholz anzünden*
strike a match

Streit D -es, **Streitigkeiten** *m* quarrel; conflict; brawl;
einen Streit beilegen settle a quarrel; *in Streit geraten*
get into a quarrel

streng B *(adj.)* hard; severe; strict; *streng bestrafen* punish severely; *streng verboten!* strictly forbidden/prohibited

Stroh D -s *n* straw

Strom A -s, ⁔e *m* [large] river; stream; current; *im Strom der Zeit* in the flow of time; *den Strom einschalten* switch on the [electric] current; *gegen den Strom schwimmen* swim against the current/stream/tide

Strumpf C -es, ⁔e *m* stocking; *die Strümpfe anziehen* put on one's stockings

Stück A -es, -e *n* piece; play; show; *in Stücke schlagen* break to pieces, smash; *ein Stück Brot* a piece/slice of bread; *pro Stück* a piece; *in einem Stück* on and on

Student B -en, -en *m* student

studieren B *(w.v.)* study; go to college; be at college

Studium D -s, -ien *n* study; studies *(pl.)*; *Studium treiben* study

Stufe B -n *f* step; stair; degree; level; *Vorsicht, Stufe!* Mind the step!; *auf gleicher Stufe mit* on a level with

Stuhl A -s, ⁔e *m* chair

Stunde A -n *f* hour; lesson; period; *eine halbe Stunde* half an hour; *stundenlang* for hours; *zur rechten Stunde* at the right moment

Sturm D -es, ⁔e *m* storm

stürmen C *(w.v.)* be stormy; take by storm; attack; *es stürmt* it blows a gale

stürzen C *(w.v.)* fall; tumble; upset; overturn; *ins Elend stürzen* ruin

suchen A *(w.v.)* seek; look for; search for; *er hat hier nichts zu suchen* he has no business here; *nach Worten suchen* be at a loss for words

Süden B -s *m* south; *im Süden* [to the] south [of]; *nach Süden* south[wards]

Summe C -n *f* sum; amount; *eine hohe Summe* a large sum/amount

Suppe B -n *f* soup

süß B *(adj.)* sweet; lovely; *süße Butter* fresh butter

Szene D **-n** *f* stage; scene

T

Tabak C **-s, -e** *m* tobacco

Tablette C **-n** *f* tablet; pill

Tafel A **-n** *f* table; blackboard; board; *eine Tafel Schokolade* a bar of chocolate

Tag A **-es, -e** *m* day; *bei Tage* during the day, by daylight; *in acht Tagen* this day week; *vor acht Tagen* a week ago; *jeden zweiten Tag* every other day; *guten Tag!* how do you do?; *tags zuvor* the day before

täglich A *(adj.)* daily

Tal B **-s, ⁓er** *n* valley

tanken C *(w.v.)* refuel; fill up

Tante B **-n** *f* aunt

Tanz C **-es, ⁓e** *m* dance; ball

Tasche A **-n** *f* pocket; bag; briefcase

Taschentuch C **-s, ⁓er** *n* handkerchief

Tasse A **-n** *f* cup; *eine Tasse Kaffee* a cup of coffee

tat → **tun**

Tat B **-en** *f* action; deed; act; achievement; *auf frischer Tat ertappen* catch red-handed; *in der Tat* in fact

tätig D *(adj.)* active; busy

Tatsache D **-n** *f* fact; data *(pl.)*

tatsächlich B *(adj.)* real; actual. *(adv.)* in fact

tausend A *(num.)* a/one thousand

Taxi C **-s, -s** *n* taxi

technisch C *(adj.)* technical

Tee C **-s, -s** *m* tea; *eine Tasse Tee* a cup of tea

Teil A **-s, -e** *m* part; share; *zum Teil* partly; *ich für meinen Teil* as for me; *ein Teil der Leute* some of the people

teilen A *(w.v.)* divide; share; *durch 3 teilen* divide by 3

teilnehmen [an] D **i/a/o** take part [in]; participate [in]

teils D *(adv.)* partly; in part

Telefon B -s, -e *n* telephone; *am Telefon* on the phone; *das Telefon bedienen* answer the phone

telefonieren B *(w.v.)* (tele)phone, ring/call up

Telegramm C -s, -e *n* telegram; message; wire

Teller B -s, - *m* plate

Temperatur C -en *f* temperature

Teppich D -s, -e *m* carpet

teuer B *(adj.)* expensive; dear; *das wird ihm teuer zu stehen kommen* he will be sorry for it yet

Theater C -s, - *n* theatre; *mach kein Theater!* don't make a fuss!

tief A *(adj.)* deep; low; *in tiefer Nacht* in the dead of night

Tier B -es, -e *n* animal; beast

Tisch A -es, -e *m* table; *bei Tisch* at dinner/table; *Gäste zu Tisch haben* have guests for dinner; *reinen Tisch machen* make a clean sweep [of it]

Tochter A ̈er *f* daughter

Tod C -es *m* death; *sich zu Tode lachen* die with laughter

Toilette D -n *f* lavatory; w.c.

toll C *(adj.)* mad; insane; *es ist zu toll* that's going too far

Ton B -s, ̈e *m* sound; tone; *der gute Ton* good form/taste

Topf A -es, ̈e *m* pot; can

Tor A -es, -e *n* gate; door; goal; *ein Tor schießen* score a goal

tot A *(adj.)* dead; *toter Punkt* deadlock

tragen A ä/u/a carry; bear; wear; *eine Brille tragen* wear glasses; *bei sich tragen* have about one

Traktor D -s, -en *m* tractor

Träne C -n *f* tear; *in Tränen ausbrechen* burst into tears

Traum B -s, ̈e *m* dream; *mein Traum ging in Erfüllung* my dream came true

traurig B *(adj.)* sad; *das Traurige daran ist ...* the sad part of it is ...

treffen A i/a/o hit; meet; *sich treffen* meet; *es trifft sich* *daß* it so happens that; *das trifft sich schlecht!* that's bad!

treiben C **ei/ie/ie** practise; carry on; go in for; *Handel treiben* do business

trennen B *(w.v.)* separate; divide [from]; *sich trennen* separate

Treppe B **-n** *f* stairs *(pl.)* ; *zwei Treppen hoch* on the second floor; *auf der Treppe* on the staircase

treten B **i/a/e** tread; step; walk; *in Kraft treten* come into force; *er tritt ins Zimmer* he enters the room

treu C *(adj.)* faithful; loyal; true

trinken A **i/a/u** drink; *Kaffee trinken* have/take coffee

Tritt D **-s, -e** *m* step; kick; *Tritt halten* keep in step

trocken A *(adj.)* dry; dull

Tropfen D **-s, -** *m* drop

Trost D **-es** *m* consolation; comfort

trotz A *(prep.)* in spite of; despite

trotzdem B *(adv.)* for all that; notwithstanding

Tuch B **-es, ⸚er** *n* cloth; fabric; scarf

tun A **u/a/a** do; perform; make; put; *tun als ob* pretend to; *er tut es ungern* he hates doing it; *es tut mir leid* I'm sorry; *hinein tun* put into; *was tut's?* what does it matter?; *das tut gut* that's a comfort

Tür A **-en** *f* door; *die Tür ist zu* the door is closed; *die Tür schließen* close/shut the door

turnen A *(w.v.)* drill; do gymnastics

U

übel B *(adj.)* evil; bad; wrong; *mir ist übel* I am/feel sick; *nicht übel* pretty good

üben B *(w.v.)* exercise; practise; train; *sich üben* practise; *Geduld üben* be patient

über A *(prep.)* over; above; across; on, upon; while, during; concerning; *den Tag über* all day long; *5 Mi-*

nuten über 3 five minutes past three

überall A *(adv.)* everywhere; over all

überhaupt B *(adv.)* at all; generally; on the whole; *überhaupt nicht* not at all

überholen D *(w.v.)* overtake; pass

übermorgen B *(adv.)* the day after tomorrow

überqueren D *(w.v.)* cross; traverse; *die Straße überqueren* cross the street

überraschen D *(w.v.)* surprise; astonish

übersetzen D *(w.v.)* translate; *aus dem Deutschen ins Englische übersetzen* translate from German into English

überzeugen D *(w.v.)* convince; persuade

übrig A *(adj.)* left [over]; remaining; rest of; *die übrigen* the others; *im übrigen* otherwise; *übrig sein* be left

übrigens C *(adv.)* moreover; besides, however; by the way

Übung C -en *f* exercise; drill; training; practice; *in der Übung bleiben* keep in training

Ufer B -s, - *n* bank; shore; beach; *am Ufer* ashore; *an den Ufern des Nils* on the banks of the Nile

Uhr A -en *f* clock; watch; *wieviel Uhr ist es?* what time it is?; *um 12 Uhr* at twelve o'clock, at noon; *die Uhr aufziehen* wind up the watch; *die Uhr geht vor* the watch is fast; *gegen 3 [Uhr]* about 3 [o'clock]; *um wieviel Uhr?* at what time?

um A *(prep.)* round; at; near; towards; by; for; *um einen Garten* around a garden; *sich ängstigen um* be worried about; *sich um 3 Uhr treffen* meet at three o'clock; *um Mitternacht* at midnight; *Jahr um Jahr* year after year

umbringen D i/a/a kill; murder; *ich hätte ihn umbringen können* I could have killed him

Umfang D -s, ⸚e *m* extent; scale; scope; circumference

umgeben D i/a/e surround

umher B *(adv.)* about; around; here and there; *rund umher* round about

umkehren B *(w.v.)* turn back; return; turn upside down; *umgekehrt* opposite, on the contrary

umsonst A *(adv.)* in vain; to no purpose; free of charge

Umstand C -s, ̈-e *m* circumstance; condition, state; *ohne Umstand* without ceremony; *unter Umständen* possibly; *unter keinen Umständen* in no circumstances; *sich Umstände machen* go to trouble

umsteigen C ei/ie/ie change (e.g. train)

um zu A in order to

unbedingt C *(adj.)* absolute; complete

und A *(conj.)* and

und so weiter A and so on

Unfall C -s, ̈-e *m* accident; disaster; misfortune

ungefähr B *(adv.)* about; around; roughly; *ungefähr 50* about 50, 50 or so

Unglück B -s *n* misfortune; accident; *zum Unglück* unfortunately

unmittelbar C *(adj.)* direct; immediate

unmöglich B *(adj.)* impossible

uns A *(pers. pron.)* [to] us

unser A *(poss. adj.)* our

unsere [-r, -s] A *(pron.)* ours

Unsinn C -s *m* nonsense; rubbish

unten A *(adv.)* below; beneath; downstairs; *da unten* down there

unter A *(prep.)* under; beneath; below, among; between; *unter der Hand* secretly; *unter uns gesagt* between you and me

unter anderem D among other things

unterbrechen D i/a/o interrupt; cut short; suspend

untergehen C e/i/a go down; sink; perish; set

unterhalten B ä/ie/a maintain; amuse, entertain; *sich unterhalten* enjoy oneself, talk to each other

Unterhaltung B -en *f* amusement; entertainment; support; conversation

unternehmen D i/a/o undertake; attempt

Unterricht B -s *m* instruction; lessons *(pl.)*; *Unterricht geben* teach

unterscheiden D ei/ie/ie distinguish

Unterschied C -s, -e *m* difference; *zum Unterschied von* as distinguished from; *ohne Unterschied* alike

unterschreiben C ei/ie/ie sign

untersuchen B *(w.v.)* examine; investigate

Untersuchung C -en *f* examination; inquiry; investigation; *ärztliche Untersuchung* medical examination

unvergleichlich D *(adj.)* incomparable; unparalleled; unique

unzufrieden B *(adj.)* dissatisfied; discontented

Urlaub C -s *m* vacation; holiday; *auf Urlaub* on leave; *Urlaub haben* be on holiday/vacation/leave

Ursache C -n *f* cause; reason; *keine Ursache!* don't mention it!

Ursprung D -s, ⸗e *m* origin; beginning

Urteil C -s, -e *n* judg(e)ment; verdict; *sich ein Urteil bilden* [*über*] form an opinion [of/on/about]

V

Vater A -s, ⸗ *m* father

verändern B *(w.v.)* change; alter; *er hat sich verändert* he has changed

verbergen C i/a/o hide; conceal; *im verborgenen* in secret

verbessern B *(w.v.)* improve; correct; *sich verbessern* better oneself

verbieten C ie/o/o forbid; prohibit; *es ist verboten* it is prohibited

verbinden B i/a/u tie together; connect; join; combine; *ich bin falsch verbunden* I've got the wrong number;

ich bin Ihnen sehr verbunden I'm very much obliged to you; *eine Wunde verbinden* dress a wound

Verbindung C -en *f* union; connection; relation; *die Verbindung verlieren mit* lose touch with

Verbrechen D -s, - *n* crime; felony

verbreiten D *(w.v.)* spread; distribute

verbrennen C e/a/a burn; scald; tan; cremate; be consumed by fire; be burnt down; *sich die Finger verbrennen* burn one's fingers

verbringen D i/a/a spend; pass; transport; *die Zeit verbringen* pass the time

verderben B i/a/o spoil; ruin; damage; *sich den Magen verderben* upset one's stomach; *verdorbenes Fleisch* tainted meat

verdienen A *(w.v.)* earn; gain; make money; deserve; *er verdient eine Belohnung* he deserves a reward

vereinigen A *(w.v.)* unite; join; unify; *die Vereinigten Staaten* the United States

Verfahren D -s, - *n* method; process

verfolgen C *(w.v.)* pursue; prosecute; follow up; *heimlich verfolgen* shadow

vergangen → **vergehen**

Vergangenheit C -en *f* past; background

vergebens D *(adv.)* in vain; vainly

vergehen B e/i/a pass; blow over; fade; perish; *mir verging die Lust dazu* I lost the liking for it; *vergangenes Jahr* last year

vergessen A i/a/e forget; overlook; *sich vergessen* forget oneself

vergleichen B ei/i/i compare; *vergleichen mit* compared to

Vergnügen B -s, - *n* pleasure; joy; *es aus Vergnügen tun* do it for fun; *viel Vergnügen!* enjoy yourself!

verhaften D *(w.v.)* arrest; *verhaftet werden* get arrested

Verhältnis C -ses, -se *n* relation; situation; ratio

Verhandlung C -en *f* negotiation; debate; *Verhandlungen aufnehmen* enter into negotiations

verheiratet B *(adj.)* married

Verkauf B **-s, ⁻e** *m* sale; *zum Verkauf* for sale

verkaufen A *(w.v.)* sell; *mit Gewinn verkaufen* sell at a profit

Verkehr B **-s** *m* traffic; *Verkehrsunfall* traffic accident

verlangen A *(w.v.)* demand; require; want; ask [for], long [for]; *das ist zu viel verlangt* that's asking too much; *was verlangen Sie von mir?* what do you want of me?

verlassen A **ä/ie/a** leave; abandon; desert; *sich verlassen auf* rely on, depend on; *Sie können sich darauf verlassen* you can count on that

verletzen C *(w.v.)* hurt; injure

verlieren A **ie/o/o** lose; waste; *den Verstand verlieren* lose one's reason

vermeiden D **ei/ie/ie** avoid; *es läßt sich nicht vermeiden* it cannot be helped

Vermögen D **-s, -** *n* ability; power; property; fortune; *nach bestem Vermögen* to the best of one's ability

vermuten D *(w.v.)* suppose; suspect; guess

vernichten C *(w.v.)* do away with; destroy; smash

vernünftig C *(adj.)* reasonable; sensible

verpassen B *(w.v.)* let slip; miss; lose by delay; *den Zug verpassen* miss the train

verpflichten [zu] B *(w.v.)* oblige [to]; engage; pledge

verrückt B *(adj.)* crazy; mad

versammeln D *(w.v.)* gather; bring together; assemble; *sich versammeln* meet

Versammlung D **-en** *f* meeting; assembly; convention; *eine Versammlung fand statt* a meeting was held

verschieden A *(adj.)* different; *zu verschiedenen Malen* on various occasions

verschließen D **ie/o/o** close; lock; shut; *sich einer Sache verschließen* shut one's eyes to something

verschwinden B **i/a/u** disappear

Versehen D -s, - *n* mistake; error; *aus Versehen* by mistake; unintentionally

versichern D *(w.v.)* assure; insure; *sich versichern* make sure of

versprechen C i/a/o promise; *sich versprechen* make a slip of the tongue

Verstand C -es *m* understanding; intellect, brains *(pl.)* reason; *nicht bei Verstand sein* be out of one's mind

verstanden → **verstehen**

verstecken C *(w.v.)* hide; conceal

verstehen A e/a/a understand; see; hear; make out; *ich verstehe!* I see!; *ich verstehe daß ...* I hear that ...

Versuch B -s, -e *m* experiment; attempt; test; *einen Versuch anstellen* set up an experiment

versuchen A *(w.v.)* attempt; try; test; taste; *sein Glück versuchen* seek one's fortune

verteidigen D *(w.v.)* defend

Vertrauen C -s *n* confidence; trust; *im Vertrauen* confidentially; *das Vertrauen verlieren zu* lose faith in

verursachen D *(w.v.)* cause; bring about; raise

vervollständigen D *(w.v.)* complete

[sich] verwandeln D *(w.v.)* change; transform; turn into

verwandt [mit] C *(adj.)* related [to]; akin [to]; *sie sind verwandt* they are related

verwechseln C *(w.v.)* exchange; mistake for; confuse

verweigern D *(w.v.)* deny; refuse

verwenden C *(w.v.)* apply; employ; use; *viel Zeit verwenden [auf]* spend a lot of time [on]

verwirklichen D *(w.v.)* realize; accomplish; *seine Träume verwirklichen* realize one's dreams

verwirren D *(w.v.)* puzzle; mix up; confuse

verwunden C *(w.v.)* wound; injure; hurt

Verzeichnis C -ses, -se *n* list; inventory; index

verzeihen C ei/ie/ie pardon; forgive; *verzeihen Sie!* excuse me!, sorry!

verzollen D *(w.v.)* pay duty on; *ich habe etwas zu verzollen* I have something to declare

Vieh D -s *n* cattle; beast

viel A *(adj.)* much; a lot of; a great deal; *so viel(e)* so much, so many; *viel besser* much better; *ziemlich viel* a good deal; *viel Glück!* good luck! *vielen Dank!* thanks a lot!

vielleicht A *(adv.)* perhaps; maybe; possibly

vielmals C *(adv.)* many times; often

vielmehr B *(adv.)* rather; much more; on the contrary

Viertel B -s, - *n* quarter; *ein Viertel vor drei* a quarter to three; *ein Viertel nach fünf* a quarter past five

Vogel B -s,⁓ *m* bird

Volk B -s,⁓er *n* people; nation; *das gemeine Volk* the ordinary people; the mob

voll A *(adj.)* full [of]; whole complete; *voll Wasser* filled with water; *in voller Fahrt* at full speed

vollenden D *(w.v.)* finish; end; close; complete; accomplish

völlig A *(adj.)* complete; entire

vollkommen C *(adj.)* perfect; accomplished

vollständig B *(adj.)* complete; entire; whole

vom = **von dem**

von A *(prep.)* of; from; by; about; *von morgen an* from tomorrow; *von wem ist das Buch?* who wrote the book?; *er erzählte von seiner Reise* he told about his journey

vor A *(prep.)* before; ago; since; to; of; in front of; from; because of; *vor allem* first of all; *nicht vor* not till; *vier Stunden vor der Zeit* four hours before time; *ein Viertel vor acht* a quarter to eight; *warnen vor* warn of/against; *vor 8 Tagen* a week ago

vor allem C *(adv.)* first of all; above all

vor kurzem C *(adv.)* the other day; recently

voraus C *(adv.)* before; ahead of; forward; *im voraus* beforehand

vorbei A *(adv.)* by; along; past; over; *es ist vorbei* it is over; *er ging mir vorbei* he passed me by

vorbereiten B *(w.v.)* prepare; get ready

Vorderseite C **-en** *f* front; face
vorgestern B *(adv.)* the day before yesterday
vorhanden C *(adj.)* available; at hand; existing; present
Vorhang D **-s, ⸚e** *m* curtain; *der Eiserne Vorhang* the Iron Curtain
vorher B *(adv.)* beforehand; in advance; previously; *kurz vorher* a short time before
vorhin B *(adv.)* before; a little while ago; just now
vorig B *(adj.)* former; last; *voriges Jahr* last year
vorläufig C *(adj.)* preliminary; temporary
Vormittag A **-s, -e** *m* morning; forenoon; *am Vormittag* in the morning; *heute Vormittag* this morning
vorn[e] B *(adv.)* before; in front; ahead; *nach vorn* forward; *von vorn nach hinten* from front to back
Vorname C **-n, -n** *m* Christian name; first name
Vorrat C **-s, ⸚e** *m* store; supply; provision
Vorschlag C **-s, ⸚e** *m* proposal
Vorsicht C *f* caution; care; precaution; *Vorsicht!* look out!
vorstellen D *(w.v.)* put forward; introduce; present; represent; *sich vorstellen* imagine; *darf ich Ihnen Herrn X vorstellen* allow me to introduce Mr X
Vorstellung D **-en** *f* performance; show; idea; imagination; introduction
Vorteil C **-s, -e** *m* advantage; benefit; *zu Ihrem Vorteil* in your interest
vorüber B *(adv.)* past; along; *es geht bald vorüber* it will soon be over
vorwärts C *(adv.)* forward; *vorwärts!* go on! forward!
vorziehen D **ie/o/o** prefer; draw [forth]
vorzüglich D *(adj.)* excellent; superior

W

Waage C **-n** *f* balance; scales *(pl.)*; *auf die Waage legen* put on the scales

wach B *(adj.)* awake; *ganz wach* wide awake; *wach werden* wake up

wachsen A **ä/u/a** grow; increase; *ans Herz wachsen* become very attached to

Waffe C **-n** *f* weapon; arm; *zu den Waffen rufen* call to arms

wagen C *(w.v.)* risk; venture; dare; stake; *wer wagt, gewinnt* nothing venture nothing gain

Wagen A **-s, -** *m* carriage; car; vehicle; *mit dem Wagen fahren* go/travel by car

Wahl C **-en** *f* choice; election; voting; *eine Wahl treffen* make a choice

wählen B *(w.v.)* choose; elect; vote; *die Nummer wählen* dial the number

wahr A *(adj.)* true; sincere; real; *nicht wahr?* don't you think so?; *wahr werden* come true

während A *(prep.)* during; while

Wahrheit B **-en** *f* truth; *die Wahrheit sagen* tell the truth

wahrscheinlich A *(adj.)* probable; likely; *wahrscheinlich ist er zu Hause* he is likely to be in

Wald A **-es, ̈er** *m* wood; forest

Wand B **̈e** *f* wall; side; *in seinen vier Wänden* at home; *mit dem Kopf gegen die Wand rennen* bang one's head against a brick wall

wandern C *(w.v.)* wander; walk; hike; roam

Wange D **-n** *f* cheek

wann A *(adv.)* when; *dann und wann* now and then; *seit wann?* how long?; *bis wann?* till when?, how soon?

war → **sein**

Ware C **-n** *f* article; product; goods *(pl.)*

waren → **sein**

warm A *(adj.)* warm; *mir ist warm* I am warm

Wärme B *f* warmth

warnen C *(w.v.)* warn; caution

warten A *(w.v.)* wait; expect; *warten lassen* keep waiting; *warten Sie hier* wait here

warum A *(adv.)* why; *warum nicht?* why not?, I don't mind

was A *(pron.)* what; that; which; *was für ein!* what a!

waschen A ä/u/a wash; *sich waschen* wash

Wäsche B *f* laundry; linen; *in die Wäsche geben* send to the laundry; *in der Wäsche sein* be at the wash

Wasser A -s, - *n* water; *ein Glas Wasser* a glass of water; *unter Wasser setzen* flood; *Wasser ziehen* leak

Watte D *f* cotton-wool; wadding

Wechsel D -s, - *m* change

wechseln D *(w.v.)* change; exchange; *die Kleider wechseln* change one's clothes

wecken C *(w.v.)* wake; awaken; call

weder . . . noch B *(conj.)* neither . . . nor

Weg A -es, -e *m* way; path; road; street; *am Wege* by the roadside; *er steht mir im Wege* he's in my way; *einen Weg einschlagen* take a road; *sich auf den Weg machen* set out; *er ging seines Weges* he went away

weg A *(adv.)* away; gone; disappeared; off; *weg da!* get out!; *er ist weg* he's gone; *er ist endlich weg* he's gone at last; *mein Hut ist weg* my hat is gone/lost

wegen A *(prep.)* because of; on account of

weh B *(adj.)* sore; painful; *es tut mir weh* it hurts me; *die Schulter tut mir weh* my shoulder hurts

wehen D *(w.v.)* blow; wave; *es weht ein starker Wind* there is a strong wind

weiblich D *(adj.)* female; feminine

weich A *(adj.)* soft; tender; *weichgekochtes Ei* soft-boiled egg

Weihnachten C *(pl.)* Christmas; *Fröhliche Weihnachten!* Merry Christmas!

weil A *(conj.)* because; since

Weile D *f* while; *eine Weile* for a while; *damit hat es
gute Weile* there's no hurry; *nach einer Weile* after a
while

Wein B *-s, -e m* wine; vine; *ein Glas Wein* a glass of wine

weinen B *(w.v.)* weep; cry; *vor Freude weinen* weep for
joy

weise C *(adj.)* wise; prudent

Weise B *-n f* way; method; *auf diese Weise* in this way

weiß → **wissen**

weiß A *(adj.)* white

weit A *(adv.)* far; wide; remote; far off; *bei weitem* by
far; *so weit* so far; *weit und breit* far and wide; *ein
weiter Weg* a long way; *von weitem* from a distance

weiter B *(adj. comp.)* farther; further; wider; further-
more; *weiter!* go on!; *nichts weiter* nothing more; *was
geschah weiter?* what happened next?; *und so weiter*
and so on; *sie will nicht weiter hier bleiben* she doesn't
want to stay any longer

weitergehen B *e/i/a* go on; continue

Weizen B *-s m* wheat

welch A *(pron.)* who; which; what; some; any; *welch ein
Glück!* what a bit of luck!

welche [-r, -s] A *(pron.)* what; which; who; that; *welcher
von beiden* which of the two

Welt A *-en f* world; *alle Welt* everybody; *auf die Welt
kommen* be born

wenden B *e/a/a* turn; *sich wenden gegen* turn towards

wenig A *(adj.)* little; few; *ein wenig* a little; *mit wenig
Worten* in a few words; *das ist zu wenig* that's too little

weniger B *(adj. comp.)* less; fewer; *nicht weniger als* no
less than; *immer weniger* less and less

wenigstens C *(adv.)* at least

wenn A *(conj.)* if; in case; when

wer A *(pron.)* who; *wer ist da?* who is it?, who is there?;
wer da? who goes there?; *wer anders?* who else?

werden A *i/u/o* become; get; grow, turn; *alt werden* grow
old; *es wird Nacht* it is growing dark; *ich werde mor-*

gen nach Berlin reisen I'm going to Berlin tomorrow;
es wird uns gesagt we are told

werfen A i/a/o throw

Werk B -s, -e *n* work; plant; mill; works;

wert B *(adj.)* worth; *es wert sein* be worth it; *es ist nicht
der Rede wert* it's not worth mentioning

Wert C -es, -e *m* value; worth; *großen Wert legen auf*
attach great importance to; *im Werte sinken* depre-
ciate

Wesen C -s, - *n* being; nature; character; personality;
mach nicht so viel Wesens davon don't make such a
fuss about it

wesentlich D *(adj.)* essential; *im wesentlichen* essentially

Westen B -s *m* west; *im Westen* in the west; *gegen/nach
Westen* westward; *im Westen der Stadt* the west-end
of town

Wetter B -s, - *n* weather; *es ist schönes Wetter* the weather
is fine; *bei schlechtem Wetter* in bad weather

wichtig B *(adj.)* important; essential; *nichts Wichtiges*
nothing of importance

widerstehen D e/a/a resist; withstand

wie A *(adv.)* what; how; like; such as; as; *wie lang* how
long; *wie oft* how often; *wie geht's* how are you; *wie
bitte* [I beg your] pardon; *wie ist es mit ...* what
about ...; *wie gewöhnlich* as usual; *er sieht wie ein
Engländer aus* he looks like an Englishman; *wie auch
[immer]* no matter how; *wie schade!* what a pity!

wieder A *(adv.)* again; *immer wieder* again and again;
hin und wieder now and then

wiederholen B *(w.v.)* repeat; say again

wiedersehen A ie/a/e see/meet again; *auf Wiedersehen!*
good-bye!, so long!

wiegen C ie/o/o weigh; *das Paket wiegt 2 Kilo* the parcel
weighs 2 kilos

Wiese B -n *f* meadow; pasture

wieso C *(adv.)* why, how so?; how do you mean?

wieviel A *(adv.)* how much?; how many?; *wieviel Uhr ist es?* what time is it?

wild B *(adj.)* wild; savage; *wild machen* enrage; *wilde Tiere* wild animals

will → **wollen**

Wille C -ns, -n *m* will; intention; *letzter Wille* last will and testament; *mit Willen* on purpose

willkommen C *(adj.)* welcome; *seien Sie willkommen!* welcome!; *willkommen heißen* welcome

willst → **wollen**

Wind B -es, -e *m* wind; breeze

winken D *(w.v.)* beckon; wave; nod; wink; *mit der Hand winken* wave one's hand

Winter B -s, - *m* winter; *im Winter* in winter

wir A *(pron.)* we

wird → **werden**

wirken C *(w.v.)* work; do; perform; produce; operate; take effect; *Wunder wirken* work wonders; *auf die Sinne wirken* affect the senses; *das Mittel wirkt* the remedy is effective

wirklich A *(adj.)* real; actual; true; genuine

Wirkung C -en *f* effect; action; *mit sofortiger Wirkung* with immediate effect; *eine Wirkung haben* produce an effect

Wirtschaft D -en *f* housekeeping; [domestic] economy; farm; *die Wirtschaft führen* keep house; *sie führt ihm die Wirtschaft* she runs his household

wischen D *(w.v.)* wipe [clean]; clean; rub; *die Tafel abwischen* wipe the blackboard

wissen A ei/u/u know; be aware of; *auswendig wissen* know by heart; *ich möchte wissen* I wonder

Wissenschaft D -en *f* science

wo A *(adv.)* where

Woche A -n *f* week; *heute in einer Woche* this day week, a week from now; *vor einer Woche* a week ago; *letzte Woche* last week

Wochenende C -s *n* week-end

Wochentag C -es, -e *m* week-day

woher A *(adv.)* from where

wohin A *(adv.)* where [to]

wohl B *(adv.)* well; *sich wohl fühlen* feel well; *ich kann wohl sagen* I dare say; *es mag wohl sein* it is very likely; *leben Sie wohl!* good-bye! *Sie sind wohl zufrieden* I suppose you are satisfied

wohnen A *(w.v.)* live; stay; dwell; *auf dem Lande wohnen* live in the country; *zur Miete wohnen bei* lodge with

Wohnung A -en *f* appartment; flat; rooms; *eine Wohnung beziehen* move in

Wolke B -n *f* cloud

Wolle C *f* wool; *aus Wolle* woollen, [made] of wool

wollen A i/o/o want; be willing; *lieber wollen* prefer; *was wollen Sie?* what do you want?

woran C *(adv.)* at/of/in what; *woran denken Sie?* what are you thinking about/of?

worauf C *(adv.)* on what?; for what?; on which?; after which; whereupon; *worauf alle gingen* whereupon all went

woraus C *(adv.)* of what?; from what?; out of which; from which; *woraus ist das gemacht?* what's it made of?

worden → **werden**

worin C *(adv.)* into which/what; with which; *worin besteht der Unterschied?* where does the difference lie?

Wort A -es,⁼er/-e *n* word; *Wort für Wort* word for word literally; *auf mein Wort* upon my word; *mit anderen Worten* in other words; *ein Wort gab das andere* one word led to another

worüber C *(adv.)* whereat; whereof; at which; over which; *worüber spricht er?* what's he talking about?

Wunde D -n *f* wound; *eine Wunde verbinden* dress a wound

wundern C *(w.v.)* wonder; *es wundert mich* I'm surprised

Wunsch A -es,⁼e *m* wish; desire; longing; *nach Wunsch*

as desired; *haben Sie noch einen Wunsch?* is there anything else you'd like?

wünschen A *(w.v.)* wish; desire; want; *was wünschen Sie?*
may I help you?; *wie Sie wünschen* as you wish; *Glück
wünschen* congratulate

wurde → **werden**

würde → **werden**

Würde D *f* dignity; honour; *unter aller Würde* beneath
contempt

würdig D *(adj.)* worthy; deserving

Wurst B ⁼e *f* sausage

Wurzel D -n *f* root; *mit der Wurzel ausreißen* uproot

wußte → **wissen**

Wüste D -n *f* waste; desert; wilderness

Wut D *f* rage; fury; madness; *er kochte vor Wut* he was
boiling with rage

Z

Zahl A -en *f* number; figure; *in großer Zahl* in large
numbers

zahlen B *(w.v.)* pay; *bar zahlen* pay [in] cash; *Ober, bitte
zahlen!* waiter, the bill, please!

zählen A *(w.v.)* count; number; *zählen auf* count on, rely
on; *seine Tage sind gezählt* his days are numbered

Zahn C -s,⁼e *m* tooth; *die Zähne putzen* brush one's teeth

zart C *(adj.)* tender; soft; delicate

Zehe D -n *f* toe; *vom Scheitel bis zur Zehe* from top to
toe

Zeichen B -s,- *n* sign; signal; *ein Zeichen geben* give a sign

zeichnen C *(w.v.)* draw; sketch

zeigen A *(w.v.)* show; point [at]; prove; *das wird sich
zeigen* that remains to be seen

Zeile D -n *f* line

Zeit A -en *f* time; age; era; *eine Zeit lang* for a time;
in kurzer Zeit shortly; *zur Zeit* at present, now; *vor*

Zeiten once upon a time; *lassen Sie sich Zeit* take your time; *die ganze Zeit* all the time

Zeitung A -en *f* (news)paper

Zelt D -s, -e *n* tent

zerbrechen B i/a/o break to pieces; smash

zerreißen B ei/i/i tear up;

zerschlagen C ä/u/a break; smash; beat to pieces

zerstören C *(w.v.)* destroy; ruin; break down

Zettel B -s, - *m* slip; note; label

Zeug A -s *n* stuff; matter, things; *dummes Zeug* nonsense

ziehen A ie/o/o pull; draw; *in den Krieg ziehen* go to war; *in die Länge ziehen* delay; put off; *in Zweifel ziehen* doubt

Ziel C -s, -e *n* aim; destination; *das Ziel treffen* hit the mark

ziemlich C *(adv.)* rather; *ziemlich weit* a rather long way [off]; *ziemlich gut* rather/pretty good

Zigarette A -n *f* cigarette

Zigarre A -n *f* cigar

Zimmer A -s, - *n* room; chamber; *das Zimmer liegt nach dem Garten* the room looks onto the garden; *Zimmer zu vermieten* room to let/rent

zittern D *(w.v.)* tremble; shake; *vor Angst zittern* tremble with fear

Zoll C -s,⸚e *m* 1. duty; customs. 2. inch

Zone D -n *f* zone

zu A *(prep.)* at; in; on; to; along with; in addition to; for; by; up to; with; *zu Fuß* on foot; *zu Bett* to bed; *zum Glück* fortunately; *3 zu 5* 3 by 5; *ab und zu* now and then; *zu viel* too much

Zucker B -s *m* sugar

zudecken B *(w.v.)* cover [up]; conceal

zuerst A *(adv.)* [at] first; first of all; to begin with

zufällig C *(adj.)* accidental; by chance; *ich war zufällig da* I happened to be there

zufrieden B *(adj.)* satisfied; content; *zufrieden sein* [*mit*] be satisfied [with]

Zug B -es, ⁔e *m* train; pulling; draught; *im Zuge* in the course of; *mit dem Zug* by train; *den Zug verpassen* miss the train

zugleich B *(adv.)* at the same time; along with; together with

zuhören B *(w.v.)* listen [to]; *hören Sie mal zu!* now listen!

Zukunft C *f* future; *für die Zukunft* for the future; *in Zukunft* in [the] future

zuletzt B *(adv.)* last; at last; finally; after all; *zuletzt kommen* arrive last

zum = **zu dem**

zumachen A *(w.v.)* close; shut

zunächst B *(adv.)* first; above all; to begin with

Zunge D -n *f* tongue

zur = **zu der**

zurück A *(adv.)* back; behind; backward(s); *warum bist du noch nicht zurück?* why haven't you come back yet?

zurückkehren D *(w.v.)* return; come back; go back

zusammen A *(adv.)* together; all together; in common

zusammensetzen C *(w.v.)* put together; compose; *sich zusammensetzen* sit down together

Zuschauer D -s, - *m* spectator; (tele)viewer; *die Zuschauer* the public, the audience

zuschließen D ie/o/o lock [up]; shut; close

Zustand C -s, ⁔e *m* condition; state; situation; *in gutem Zustand* in good shape

Zutritt D -s *m* access; admission; *kein Zutritt!* no admittance!

zuviel B *(adj.)* too much; *viel zuviel* far too much

zuweilen D *(adv.)* sometimes; occasionally

zwar B *(adv.)* indeed; to be sure; it is true; *und zwar* namely

Zweck B -s, -e *m* purpose; aim; goal; object; point; *keinen Zweck haben* be of no use; *zu dem Zweck* for the purpose of; *zu diesem Zweck* for this purpose; *seinen Zweck erreichen* achieve one's aim

Zweifel D -s, - *m* doubt; *in Zweifel ziehen* call in question

zweifeln D *(w.v.)* doubt; *ich zweifle nicht daran* I don't doubt it

Zweig C -es, -e *m* branch; twig

zwingen B i/a/u force; compel

zwischen A *(prep.)* between; *es ist ein Unterschied zwischen ihm und mir* there is a difference between him and me

Cardinal numbers

1	eins	20	zwanzig
2	zwei	21	einundzwanzig
3	drei	22	zweiundzwanzig
4	vier		etc.
5	fünf	30	dreißig
6	sechs	40	vierzig
7	sieben	50	fünfzig
8	acht	60	sechzig
9	neun	70	siebzig
10	zehn	80	achtzig
11	elf	90	neunzig
12	zwölf	100	hundert (einhundert)
13	dreizehn	200	zweihundert
14	vierzehn		etc.
15	fünfzehn	1000	tausend (eintausend)
16	sechzehn	2000	zweitausend
17	siebzehn		etc.
18	achtzehn		
19	neunzehn		

Ordinal numbers

der (die, das) der (die, das)

erste	elfte	dreißigste
zweite	zwölfte	vierzigste
dritte	dreizehnte	fünfzigste
vierte	vierzehnte	sechzigste
fünfte	fünfzehnte	siebzigste
sechste	sechzehnte	achtzigste
siebente	siebzehnte	neunzigste
achte	achtzehnte	hundertste
neunte	neunzehnte	
zehnte	zwanzigste	
	einundzwanzigste	
	zweiundzwanzigste	
	etc.	

The days of the week

Sonntag	Sunday
Montag	Monday
Dienstag	Tuesday
Mittwoch	Wednesday
Donnerstag	Thursday
Freitag	Friday
Sonnabend ⎫ Samstag ⎭	Saturday

The months of the year

Januar	January
Februar	February
März	March
April	April
Mai	May
Juni	June
Juli	July
August	August
September	September
Oktober	October
November	November
Dezember	December

Weights and Measures

1mm	Millimeter	=	0,1 Zentimeter	= 0.0393 inch
1 cm	Zentimeter	=	10 Millimeter	= 0.3937 inch
1 m	Meter	=	100 Zentimeter	= 1.0936 yard
1 km	Kilometer	=	1000 Meter	= 0.6213 mile

1 inch	=	2,54 cm
1 foot	=	30,48 cm
1 yard	=	0,91 m
1 mile	=	1,61 km

1 g	Gramm	=		0.04 oz
1 kg	Kilogramm	= 1000 Gramm	=	2.205 lb
1 t	Tonne(n)	= 1000 Kilogramm	=	2240 lb

1 oz	=	28,35 g
1 lb	=	0,453 kg

Abbreviations

Abb.	= Abbildung	jun., jr.	= junior (der Jüngere)
Abg.	= Abgeordneter	Kap.	= Kapitel
Abs.	= Absatz, Absender	kath.	= katholisch
A.D.	= Anno Domini	l.J.	= laufenden Jahres
	(im Jahr des Herrn)	l.M.	= laufenden Monats
Anm.	= Anmerkung	M.d.B.	= Mitglied des Bun-
Art.	= Artikel		destags (auch Mdb)
Bem.	= Bermerkung	m.E.	= meines Erachtens
betr.	= betreffend, betreffs	n.Chr.	= nach Christus
bez.	= bezahlt, bezüglich		(Christo)
b.w.	= bitte wenden	n.J.	= nächsten Jahres
bzw.	= beziehungsweise	Nr., No.	= Nummer, Numero
ca.	= zirka (ungefähr, rund)	o.B.	= ohne Befund
Co., Cie.	= Kompanie, Gesell-	Pfd.	= Pfund
	schaft	PS	= Postskriptum
desgl.	= desgleichen		(Nachschrift),
dgl.	= dergleichen		Pferdestärke
d.h.	= das heißt	s.	= siehe (s.o.=siehe
d.i.	= das ist		oben, s.u.=siehe
d.J.	= dieses Jahres		unten)
d.M.	= dieses Monats	sen.	= Senior (der Ältere)
do.	= ditto (desgleichen)	Skt., St.	= Sankt (heilig)
Dr.	= Doktor	S.	= Seite
ebd.	= ebenda	stud.	= Studiosus, Student
etc.	= et cetera (und so	u.A.w.g.	= um Antwort wird
	weiter)		gebeten
ev.	= evangelisch	u.	= und
e.V.	= eingetragener Verein	u.ä.	= und ähnliche
evtl.	= eventuell	u.a.m.	= und anderes mehr
gefl.	= gefällig	usf.	= und so fort
G.m.b.H.	= Gesellschaft mit be-	usw.	= und so weiter
	schränkter Haftung	u.U.	= unter Umständen
g.R.	= gegen Rückgabe	u.v.a.	= und viele andere
inkl.	= inklusive (ein-	v.Chr.	= vor Christus (Christo)
	schliesslich)	v.M.	= vorigen Monats
		z.B.	= zum Beispiel
		z.Z.	= zur Zeit

Countries and their inhabitants

The nation	The male inhabitant	The female inhabitant	The adjective*
Albanien	der Albanier	die Albanierin	albanisch
Amerika/die Vereinigten Staaten	- Amerikaner	- Amerikanerin	amerikanisch
Argentinien	- Argentinier	- Argentinierin	argentinisch
Belgien	- Belgier	- Belgierin	belgisch
Brasilien	- Brasilianer	- Brasilianerin	brasilianisch
Bulgarien	- Bulgare	- Bulgarin	bulgarisch
China	- Chinese	- Chinesin	chinesisch
Dänemark	- Däne	- Dänin	dänisch
Deutschland	- Deutsche	- Deutsche	deutsch
England	- Engländer	- Engländerin	englisch
Finnland	- Finne	- Finnin	finnisch
Frankreich	- Franzose	- Französin	französisch
Griechenland	- Grieche	- Griechin	griechisch
Holland	- Holländer	- Holländerin	holländisch
Indien	- Inder	- Inderin	indisch
Irland	- Irländer	- Irländerin	irländisch
Island	- Isländer	- Isländerin	isländisch
Italien	- Italiener	- Italienerin	italienisch
Japan	- Japaner	- Japanerin	japanisch
Jugoslawien	- Jugoslawe	- Jugoslawin	jugoslawisch
Kanada	- Kanadier	- Kanadierin	kanadisch
Luxemburg	- Luxemburger	- Luxemburgerin	luxemburgisch
die Niederlande	- Niederländer	- Niederländerin	niederländisch
Norwegen	- Norweger	- Norwegerin	norwegisch
Österreich	- Österreicher	- Österreicherin	österreichisch
Polen	- Pole	- Polin	polnisch
Portugal	- Portugiese	- Portugiesin	portugiesisch
Rumänien	- Rumäne	- Rumänin	rumänisch
Rußland	- Russe	- Russin	russisch
Schweden	- Schwede	- Schwedin	schwedisch
die Schweiz	- Schweizer	- Schweizerin	schweizer(isch)
Spanien	- Spanier	- Spanierin	spanisch
die Tschechoslowakei	- Tscheche	- Tschechin	tschechisch
die Türkei	- Türke	- Türkin	türkisch
Ungarn	- Ungar	- Ungarin	ungarisch

* The language spoken in each country (where applicable) is the same as the adjective: e.g. *er spricht gut deutsch*
er spricht ein gutes deutsch

Grammar

Contents

Cases

Nominative

Used (a) for the subject of a sentence

e.g. **Der Vater* ist groß†, die Mutter ist klein, das Kind ist sehr klein**

(b) after **sein, werden, bleiben, heißen** (the complement)

e.g. **Der Vater ist ein Mann, die Mutter ist eine Frau, und das Kind ist ein Mädchen**

Er wurde ein berühmter Arzt und blieb mein treuer Freund

Accusative

Used (a) for the direct object

e.g. **Der Vater putzt den Wagen, die Mutter hält eine Blume, und das Kind liest ein Buch**

(b) to show duration of time

e.g. **Die Sonne scheint den ganzen Tag** (all day)

Er arbeitete eine Stunde (for an hour)

(c) to show distance covered

e.g. **Er läuft eine Meile** (for a mile)

Das Brett war nur einen Fuß breit (only a foot wide)

(d) to show definite time

e.g. **Jeden Samstag spielt er Fußball** (every Saturday)

Letztes Jahr fuhr er nach Deutschland (last year)

(e) with certain prepositions (see pp 151—2)

e.g. **Die Familie sitzt um den Tisch**

Er lief die Straße entlang

(f) to show direction up or down

e.g. **Er steigt den steilen Weg hinauf** (up the steep path)

Er rutscht die Treppe hinunter (down the steps)

---

*N.B. All nouns in German have capital letters.

†N.B. The German **ß**(ss) symbol is used

(i) at the end of a word, e.g. **muß, Schluß**

(ii) before a third consonant, e.g. **mußte, Schloßpark**

(iii) between two vowels when the first one is long, e.g. **schließen, etwas Großes**

Genitive

(See N.B. i, below)

Used (a) to show possession

e.g. **Der Wagen des Vaters ist blau, die Blume der Mutter ist rot, und das Buch des Kindes ist grün**

(b) to show indefinite time

e.g. **Eines Tages besuchte er seine Tante** (one day)
Eines Morgens stand er früh auf (one morning)

(c) with certain prepositions (see p 151)

e.g. **Trotz des Wetters geht er spazieren**
Der Bauernhof liegt unweit des Dorfes

Dative

(See N.B. ii, below)

Used (a) for the indirect object

e.g. **Der Vater gibt dem Kind eine Puppe**
Er schreibt seiner Mutter einen Brief

(b) with certain prepositions (see pp 151—2)

e.g. **Er kommt aus dem Haus**
Er wohnt der Kirche gegenüber

(c) to show possession (normally parts of the body only)
(See also reflexive verbs p 133)

e.g. **Ich wasche mir das Gesicht**
Er klopft seinem Freund auf die Schulter

(d) with certain verbs (see p 135)

e.g. **Der Hund folgt der Katze**
Ich helfe meiner Mutter beim Abwaschen

N.B. (i) Masculine and neuter nouns add -*s* or -*es* in the genitive singular

e.g. **Der Wagen des Vaters**
In der Mitte des Marktplatzes
Die Bücher des Kindes

(ii) All nouns in the dative plural must end in -*n* except those forming their plural with -*s*

e.g. **Die Kinder sind in den Zimmern**
In den Flugzeugen sind 36 Sitzplätze
Die Kinder spielen in den Parks

(iii) Nouns and pronouns in apposition must be in the same case (see p 170)

e.g. **Hier ist mein Bruder, der Fußballspieler**

Kennst du meinen Bruder, den Fußballspieler?

Hier ist ein Bild meines Bruders, des Fußballspielers

Ich sprach mit meinem Bruder, dem Fußballspieler

Articles

The definite article (the)

	M.	*F.*	*N.*	*Pl.*
N.	der	die	das	die
A.	den	die	das	die
G.	des	der	des	der
D.	dem	der	dem	den

The indefinite article (a, an)

	M.	*F.*	*N.*
N.	ein	eine	ein
A.	einen	eine	ein
G.	eines	einer	eines
D.	einem	einer	einem

The negative article (not a, no, not any)
nicht ein = kein

	M.	*F.*	*N.*	*Pl.*
N.	kein	keine	kein	keine
A.	keinen	keine	kein	keine
G.	keines	keiner	keines	keiner
D.	keinem	keiner	keinem	keinen

Demonstrative adjectives

(a) *Stems*

dies- this   manch- many a, many

jed- each, every   solch- such

jen- that   welch- which

(b) *Endings*   e.g. **Dieses Mädchen wohnt in jenem Haus.**

	M.	F.	N.	Pl.
N.	**-ER**	**-E**	**-ES**	**-E**
A.	**-EN**	**-E**	**-ES**	**-E**
G.	**-ES**	**-ER**	**-ES**	**-ER**
D.	**-EM**	**-ER**	**-EM**	**-EN**

Derselbe (the same)

	M.	F.	N.	Pl.
N.	derselbe	dieselbe	dasselbe	dieselben
A.	denselben	dieselbe	dasselbe	dieselben
G.	desselben	derselben	desselben	derselben
D.	demselben	derselben	demselben	denselben

USES OF THE ARTICLES, ETC

Contractions of the definite article

The following are the more common contractions:

an das — ans	in dem — im
an dem — am	um das — ums
auf das — aufs	von dem — vom
bei dem — beim	zu dem — zum
in das — ins	zu der — zur

The contracted form is used when we do not wish to stress the definite article. It should be used in the following cases:

am Tag by day
am Sonntag usw on Sunday etc.
im allgemeinen generally
im Gegenteil on the contrary
im Sommer usw in summer etc.
im Juli usw in July etc.
zum Beispiel for example
er hat Sie zum besten he is pulling your leg

Special uses of the definite article

(i) Often before abstract nouns or nouns used in a generalised sense

e.g. **Die Natur** nature   **Das Schicksal** fate
Der Mensch ist sterblich Man is mortal
Das Eisen ist ein Metall Iron is a metal

(ii) Instead of the possessive adjective with parts of the body or with clothing when it is clear to whom they belong

e.g. **Er steckte die Hand in die Tasche.   Ich wasche mir das Gesicht**

(iii) Before the names of countries if they are feminine or plural

e.g. **Die Schweiz.   Die Vereinigten Staaten**

(iv) Before the names of rivers or mountains

e.g. **Die Mosel.   Der Taunus.   Köln liegt am Rhein.**
Die Jungfrau ist ein berühmter Berg

(v) Where English omits the article with days, months, seasons and meals after a preposition

e.g. **Am Montag** on Monday   **Im Frühling** in Spring
Im August in August   **Nach dem Mittagessen** after
lunch

(vi) With proper nouns preceded by an adjective

e.g. **Der kleine Hans.   Das heutige Deutschland**

(vii) Before names of streets etc.

e.g. **Meine Freunde haben eine Wohnung in der Sallstraße**
Das Theater liegt am Deinhardplatz

(viii) Where English uses the indefinite article in expressions of price, quantity etc.

e.g. **Die Trauben kosten eine Mark das Pfund** (one mark a pound)

(ix) In certain stock phrases
ins Ausland, im Ausland abroad
in der Schule in school
in der Stadt in town
im Bett in bed
aus dem Bett out of bed
in der Tat in fact
zum Beispiel for example
mit der Bahn usw by train etc.
in die Schule, Kirche gehen to go to school, church

Omission of the indefinite article

(i)   After **sein, werden, bleiben** and **heißen** before nouns denoting a profession or nationality, unless there is a defining adjective

e.g. **Er ist Arzt** He is a doctor.

   Er ist ein guter Arzt He is a good doctor.

(ii) In certain stock phrases

e.g. **Er hat guten Appetit** He has a good appetite.

   Er hat Fieber He has a temperature.

   Er hat Kopfschmerzen He has a headache.

   Wir haben Besuch We have a visitor.

   Er hat Eile He is in a hurry.

   Mit leiser (lauter) Stimme In a quiet (loud) voice.

   Es ist schade It's a pity.

   Zu Ende kommen To come to an end.

Some, Any (singular)

There is no equivalent of the French partitive article

e.g. **Ich habe Brot** I have some bread.

   Ich habe keine Milch I have no milk.

Verbs

Persons

	Singular	Plural
First	**ich** I	**wir** we
Second familiar	**du** you	**ihr** you
Third masculine	**er** he, it	
feminine	**sie** she, it	**sie** they
neuter	**es** it	
Second polite	**Sie** you	**Sie** you

The familiar form is used
(a) among relatives, e.g. **Er fragt seinen Vater: ,,Hast du mein Buch?"**
(b) among close friends, e.g. **Er sagt seinem alten Freund: ,,Du siehst krank aus."**
(c) among children, e.g. **Karl fragt Peter: ,,Siehst du den roten Wagen?"**
(d) by an adult talking to children, e.g. **Der Lehrer sagt: ,,Ihr seid artige Kinder."**

TENSES (indicative)

Present (e.g. **spielen** to play)

Formed by adding the following endings to the verb stem (**spiel-**).

Singular			Plural		
ich	**-E**	(spiele)	**wir**	**-EN**	(spielen)
du	**-ST**	(spielst)	**ihr**	**-T**	(spielt)
er, sie, es	**-T**	(spielt)	**sie**	**-EN**	(spielen)
Sie	**-EN**	(spielen)	**Sie**	**-EN**	(spielen)

N.B. (i) Some strong verbs change their stem vowel in the second familiar and third persons singular, e.g. **tragen: du trägst, geben: er gibt.**
(ii) Verbs with stems ending in **-d, -t, chn, -ckn, -dn, -fn, -gn** or **-tn** retain the *-e* of the first person singular throughout, e.g. **du arbeitest, er öffnet.**

Imperfect

Weak verbs (e.g. **spielen**)

Add the following endings to the stem (**spiel-**).

Singular			Plural		
ich	-TE	(spielte)	wir	-TEN	(spielten)
du	-TEST	(spieltest)	ihr	-TET	(spieltet)
er, sie, es	-TE	(spielte)	sie	-TEN	(spielten)
Sie	-TEN	(spielten)	Sie	-TEN	(spielten)

Strong verbs (e.g. **geben** to give)

(a) *Stem.* Strong verbs change their stem vowel and sometimes the whole stem. These new forms must be learned (see pp 123—7).

(b) *Endings.* Add the following endings to this new stem (**gab-**).

Singular			Plural		
ich		(gab)	wir	-EN	(gaben)
du	-ST	(gabst)	ihr	-T	(gabt)
er, sie, es		(gab)	sie	-EN	(gaben)
Sie	-EN	(gaben)	Sie	-EN	(gaben)

Perfect

(a) *Formation*

Formed by using the present tense of **haben** or **sein** and the past participle

N.B. This past participle goes to the end of the clause (see p 164)

(b) ***Haben* or *sein*?**

Haben is used

(i) with all transitive verbs,

e.g. **Ich habe den Mann gesehen. Er hat das Buch gekauft**

(ii) with intransitive verbs which do not show a change of state or place,

e.g. **Es hat heute geregnet. Die Sonne hat den ganzen Tag geschienen**

Sein is used with intransitive verbs showing a change of place (e.g. **gehen**) or state (e.g. **einschlafen**),

e.g. **Er ist in die Stadt gegangen. Ich bin um 4 Uhr eingeschlafen**

(c) *The past participle*

(i) *Weak verbs.* Add **ge-** to the front of the stem and **-(e)t** to the end

e.g. **machen—gemacht   spielen—gespielt   baden—gebadet
atmen—geatmet**

(ii) *Strong verbs.* Like the imperfect stems these must be learned (see pp 123—7)

(iii) *Compound verbs* (see p 132). If the prefix is separable add it to the full past participle of the verb

e.g. **aufgehen—aufgegangen   untergehen—untergegangen**

If the prefix is inseparable there is no **ge-**

e.g. **besprechen—besprochen   empfehlen—empfohlen**

(iv) *Verbs ending in -ieren*

These verbs have no **ge-** in the past participle

e.g. **probieren—probiert   reparieren—repariert**

(v) *Modal verbs*

See page 131, note iv

N.B. The following verbs which take **sein**

abbiegen to turn off (from a road)	**Er ist vom Wege abgebogen**
aufbrechen to set out	**Wir sind um 4 Uhr aufgebrochen**
aufstehen to stand, get up	**Ich bin um 7 Uhr aufgestanden**
aufwachen to wake up	**Er ist um 3 Uhr aufgewacht**
begegnen to meet (see p 135)	**Er ist dem Mann begegnet**
bleiben to stay	**Du bist zu Hause geblieben**
einfallen to occur to (see p 135)	**Es ist mir eingefallen, daß ...**
folgen to follow (see p 135)	**Der Hund ist seinem Herrn gefolgt**
gelingen to succeed (see p 135)	**Es ist mir gelungen, das Rätsel zu lösen**
geschehen to happen	**Ein Unfall ist geschehen**
kentern to capsize	**Das Boot ist gekentert**
klettern to climb (intrans.)	**Wir sind auf die Berge geklettert**
passieren to happen	**Nichts Wichtiges ist passiert**
reisen to travel	**Er ist nach Deutschland gereist**

sein to be (see pp 121, 122)	**Ich bin in Deutschland gewesen**	
stürzen to rush, fall	**Er ist aus dem Haus gestürzt**	
umziehen to move (house)	**Die Familie ist neulich umgezogen**	
verreisen to go away	**Er ist auf zwei Tage verreist**	
verunglücken to have an accident	**Er ist tödlich verunglückt**	
vorkommen to happen	**Das ist nur selten vorgekommen**	

The pluperfect

Formed by using the imperfect of **haben** or **sein** and the past participle
e.g. **Ich hatte den Mann gesehen.   Er war in die Stadt gegangen**

Future

Formed by using the present tense of **werden** (see p 122) and the infinitive. N.B. This infinitive goes to the end of the clause
e.g. **Ich werde in die Stadt gehen. Du wirst ein Buch kaufen.**

If the future idea is contained elsewhere in the clause, the present not the future tense is normally used
e.g. **Nächstes Jahr fahre ich nach Deutschland**

SEIN, HABEN AND WERDEN

Indicative

	Present	*Imperfect*	*Perfect*	*Pluperfect*
Sein				
ich	bin	war	ist gewesen	war gewesen
du	bist	warst	etc.	etc.
er, sie, es	ist	war		
wir	sind	waren		
ihr	seid	wart		
sie, Sie	sind	waren		

	Present	*Imperfect*	*Perfect*	*Pluperfect*
Haben				
ich	habe	hatte	habe gehabt	hatte gehabt
du	hast	hattest	etc.	etc.
er, sie, es	hat	hatte		
wir	haben	hatten		
ihr	habt	hattet		
sie, Sie	haben	hatten		

Werden				
ich	werde	wurde	bin geworden	war geworden
du	wirst	wurdest	etc.	etc.
er, sie, es	wird	wurde		
wir	werden	wurden		
ihr	werdet	wurdet		
sie, Sie	werden	wurden		

Subjunctive

Sein				
ich	sei	wäre	sei gewesen	wäre gewesen
du	seiest	wärest	etc.	etc.
er, sie, es	sei	wäre		
wir	seien	wären		
ihr	seiet	wäret		
sie, Sie	seien	wären		

Haben				
ich	habe	hätte	habe gehabt	hätte gehabt
du	habest	hättest	etc.	etc.
er, sie, es	habe	hätte		
wir	haben	hätten		
ihr.	habet	hättet		
sie, Sie	haben	hätten		

	Present	Imperfect	Perfect	Pluperfect
Werden				
ich	werde	würde	sei geworden	wäre geworden
du	werdest	würdest	etc.	etc.
er, sie, es	werde	würde		
wir	werden	würden		
ihr	werdet	würdet		
sie, Sie	werden	würden		

Strong and irregular weak verbs

N.B. This list is not complete but contains most of the common verbs.

Infinitive	3rd pers. Present	3rd pers. Imperfect	3rd pers. Perfect	Meaning
backen	bäckt	buk	hat gebacken	to bake
befehlen	befiehlt	befahl	hat befohlen	order
beginnen	beginnt	begann	hat begonnen	begin
bergen	birgt	barg	hat geborgen	shelter
beißen	beißt	biß	hat gebissen	bite
biegen	biegt	bog	hat gebogen	bend, turn
bieten	bietet	bot	hat geboten	offer
binden	bindet	band	hat gebunden	tie
bitten	bittet	bat	hat gebeten	ask
blasen	bläst	blies	hat geblasen	blow
bleiben	bleibt	blieb	ist geblieben	stay
braten	brät	briet	hat gebraten	roast
brechen	bricht	brach	hat gebrochen	break (transitive)
			ist gebrochen	break (intr)
brennen	brennt	brannte	hat gebrannt	burn
bringen	bringt	brachte	hat gebracht	bring
denken	denkt	dachte	hat gedacht	think
empfehlen	empfiehlt	empfahl	hat empfohlen	recommend
erschrecken	erschrickt	erschrak	ist erschrocken	be frightened

B

essen	ißt	aß	hat gegessen	eat
fahren	fährt	fuhr	ist gefahren	go (by vehicle) (intr)
			hat gefahren	drive (transitive)
fallen	fällt	fiel	ist gefallen	fall
fangen	fängt	fing	hat gefangen	catch
finden	findet	fand	hat gefunden	find
fliegen	fliegt	flog	ist geflogen	fly
fliehen	flieht	floh	ist geflohen	flee
fließen	fließt	floß	ist geflossen	flow
fressen	frißt	fraß	hat gefressen	eat (of animals)
frieren	friert	fror	hat gefroren	freeze, be cold
geben	gibt	gab	hat gegeben	give
gehen	geht	ging	ist gegangen	go, walk
gelingen	gelingt	gelang	ist gelungen	succeed
gelten	gilt	galt	hat gegolten	be valid, worth
genießen	genießt	genoß	hat genossen	enjoy
geschehen	geschieht	geschah	ist geschehen	happen
gewinnen	gewinnt	gewann	hat gewonnen	win
gießen	gießt	goß	hat gegossen	pour
gleiten	gleitet	glitt	ist geglitten	slide
graben	gräbt	grub	hat gegraben	dig
greifen	greift	griff	hat gegriffen	seize
haben	hat	hatte	hat gehabt	have
halten	hält	hielt	hat gehalten	hold, stop (intr)
hängen	hängt	hing	hat gehangen	hang (intr)
heben	hebt	hob	hat gehoben	raise
heißen	heißt	hieß	hat geheißen	be called
helfen	hilft	half	hat geholfen	help
kennen	kennt	kannte	hat gekannt	know (people, places)

klingen	klingt	klang	hat geklungen	sound
kommen	kommt	kam	ist gekommen	come
kriechen	kriecht	kroch	ist gekrochen	creep
laden	lädt	lud	hat geladen	load
lassen	läßt	ließ	hat gelassen	leave
laufen	läuft	lief	ist gelaufen	run
leiden	leidet	litt	hat gelitten	suffer
leihen	leiht	lieh	hat geliehen	lend
lesen	liest	las	hat gelesen	read
liegen	liegt	lag	hat gelegen	lie
lügen	lügt	log	hat gelogen	tell lies
messen	mißt	maß	hat gemessen	measure
nehmen	nimmt	nahm	hat genommen	take
nennen	nennt	nannte	hat genannt	name
pfeifen	pfeift	pfiff	hat gepfiffen	whistle
preisen	preist	pries	hat gepriesen	praise
raten	rät	riet	hat geraten	advise, guess
reiben	reibt	rieb	hat gerieben	rub
reißen	reißt	riß	hat gerissen	tear
reiten	reitet	ritt	ist geritten	ride (horse, etc.) (intr)
			hat geritten	ride (transitive)
rennen	rennt	rannte	ist gerannt	run
riechen	riecht	roch	hat gerochen	smell
rinnen	rinnt	rann	ist geronnen	flow, trickle
rufen	ruft	rief	hat gerufen	call, shout
saugen	saugt	sog	hat gesogen	suck
schaffen	schafft	schuf	hat geschaffen	create
scheinen	scheint	schien	hat geschienen	seem, shine
schelten	schilt	schalt	hat gescholten	blame, scold
schieben	schiebt	schob	hat geschoben	push
schießen	schießt	schoß	hat geschossen	shoot
schlafen	schläft	schlief	hat geschlafen	sleep
schlagen	schlägt	schlug	hat geschlagen	hit
schleichen	schleicht	schlich	ist geschlichen	creep

schließen	schließt	schloß	hat geschlossen	
				shut
schmeißen	schmeißt	schmiß	hat geschmissen	
				fling
schmelzen	schmilzt	schmolz	hat geschmolzen	
				melt (trans)
			ist geschmolzen	
				melt (intr)
schneiden	schneidet	schnitt	hat geschnitten	
				cut
schreiben	schreibt	schrieb	hat geschrieben	
				write
schreien	schreit	schrie	hat geschrie(e)n	
				shout, scream
schreiten	schreitet	schritt	ist geschritten	
				stride
schweigen	schweigt	schwieg	hat geschwiegen	
				say nothing
schwimmen	schwimmt	schwamm	hat geschwommen	
				swim
schwingen	schwingt	schwang	hat geschwungen	
				swing
schwören	schwört	schwur	hat geschworen	
				swear, vow
sehen	sieht	sah	hat gesehen	see
sein	ist	war	ist gewesen	be
senden	sendet	sandte	hat gesandt	send
		sendete	hat gesendet	
singen	singt	sang	hat gesungen	sing
sinken	sinkt	sank	ist gesunken	sink (intr)
sitzen	sitzt	saß	hat gesessen	be sitting
speien	speit	spie	hat gespie(e)n	spit
sprechen	spricht	sprach	hat gesprochen	
				speak
springen	springt	sprang	ist gesprungen	jump
stechen	sticht	stach	hat gestochen	prick, sting
stehen	steht	stand	hat gestanden	stand

126

stehlen	stiehlt	stahl	hat gestohlen	steal
steigen	steigt	stieg	ist gestiegen	climb
sterben	stirbt	starb	ist gestorben	die
stoßen	stößt	stieß	hat gestoßen	push
streiten	streitet	stritt	hat gestritten	argue
tragen	trägt	trug	hat getragen	carry, wear
treffen	trifft	traf	hat getroffen	meet, hit
treiben	treibt	trieb	hat getrieben	drive, go in for
treten	tritt	trat	ist getreten	tread, step
trinken	trinkt	trank	hat getrunken	drink
tun	tut	tat	hat getan	do
verderben	verdirbt	verdarb	hat verdorben	spoil
vergessen	vergißt	vergaß	hat vergessen	forget
verlieren	verliert	verlor	hat verloren	lose
vermeiden	vermeidet	vermied	hat vermieden	avoid
ver- schwinden	ver- schwindet	ver- schwand	ist verschwunden	disappear
verzeihen	verzeiht	verzieh	hat verziehen	pardon
wachsen	wächst	wuchs	ist gewachsen	grow
waschen	wäscht	wusch	hat gewaschen	wash
weisen	weist	wies	hat gewiesen	point, show
wenden	wendet	wandte	hat gewandt	turn (trans.)
		wendete	hat gewendet	
werden	wird	wurde	ist geworden	become
werfen	wirft	warf	hat geworfen	throw
wiegen	wiegt	wog	hat gewogen	weigh (intr)
winden	windet	wand	hat gewunden	twist, wind
wissen*	weiß	wußte	hat gewußt	know (facts)
ziehen	zieht	zog	hat gezogen	pull
			ist gezogen	go, move
zwingen	zwingt	zwang	hat gezwungen	force

*wissen present tense: **ich weiß, du weißt, er weiß, wir wissen, ihr wißt, sie wissen.**

21

SUBJUNCTIVE

Present tense (e.g. **spielen**)

Formed by adding the following endings to the stem (**spiel-**).

Singular			Plural		
ich	-E	(spiele)	wir	-EN	(spielen)
du	-EST	(spielest)	ihr	-ET	(spielet)
er, sie, es	-E	(spiele)	sie	-EN	(spielen)
Sie	-EN	(spielen)	Sie	-EN	(spielen)

N.B. Strong verbs do not change their stem vowel.

e.g. **Er gebe, du sprechest**

Imperfect tense

(i) *Weak verbs* (e.g. **spielen**)

Add the following endings to the stem.

Singular			Plural		
ich	-TE	(spielte)	wir	-TEN	(spielten)
du	-TEST	(spieltest)	ihr	-TET	(spieltet)
er, sie, es	-TE	(spielte)	sie	-TEN	(spielten)
Sie	-TEN	(spielten)	Sie	-TEN	(spielten)

N.B. This is the same as the imperfect indicative.

(ii) *Strong verbs* (e.g. **geben**)

Formed by adding the following endings to the 3rd person singular imperfect indicative and by adding an umlaut to the stem vowel (**gäb-**).

Singular			Plural		
ich	-E	(gäbe)	wir	-EN	(gäben)
du	-EST	(gäbest)	ihr	-ET	(gäbet)
er, sie, es	-E	(gäbe)	sie	-EN	(gäben)
Sie	-EN	(gäben)	Sie	-EN	(gäben)

Perfect and pluperfect

Formed in the same way as the indicative except that the subjunctive forms of the auxiliary verbs are used (see pp 122, 123)

e.g. **Er sei in die Stadt gegangen**

Er hätte Fußball gespielt

Future

Formed in the same way as the indicative except that the present subjunctive of **werden** is used (see p 123)

e.g. **Du werdest in die Stadt gehen**
   Er werde Fußball spielen

Modals

Form their subjunctives like regular weak verbs.

e.g. **Du solltest in die Stadt gehen**
   Er könnte Fußball spielen

Uses of the subjunctive

(i)   In indirect speech and question (see p 162)
(ii) In some conditional clauses (see p 163)
(iii) After **als ob** (as if).
(iv) In exclamatory wishes, e.g. **Lang lebe die Königin!**
(v)   Sometimes after the conjunction **damit** in the past,
e.g. **Er stand auf, damit wir ihn sehen könnten.**

MODAL VERBS

	Dürfen to be allowed to	**Können** to be able to	**Mögen** to like, want to
Present Indic.			
ich	**darf**	**kann**	**mag**
du	**darfst**	**kannst**	**magst**
er, sie, es	**darf**	**kann**	**mag**
wir	**dürfen**	**können**	**mögen**
ihr	**dürft**	**könnt**	**mögt**
sie, Sie	**dürfen**	**können**	**mögen**
Present Subjunc.			
ich	**dürfe**	**könne**	**möge**

Imperfect Indic.

ich	durfte	konnte	mochte

Imp. Subjunc.

ich	dürfte	könnte	möchte

Perfect Indic.

ich habe	(i) **gedurft**	(i) **gekonnt**	(i) **gemocht**
	(ii) **dürfen***	(ii) **können***	(ii) **mögen***

Future Indic.

ich werde	dürfen	können	mögen

	Müssen to have to	**Sollen** to ought to	**Wollen** to want to	**Lassen†** to let, allow
Present Indic.				
ich	muß	soll	will	lasse
du	mußt	sollst	willst	läßt
er, sie, es	muß	soll	will	läßt
wir	müssen	sollen	wollen	lassen
ihr	müßt	sollt	wollt	laßt
sie, Sie	müssen	sollen	wollen	lassen
Present Subjunc.				
ich	müsse	solle	wolle	lasse
Imperfect Indic.				
ich	mußte	sollte	wollte	ließ
Imp. Subjunc.				
ich	müßte	sollte	wollte	ließe
Perfect Indic.				
ich habe	(i) **ge-mußt**	(i) **ge-sollt**	(i) **ge-wollt**	(i) **ge-lassen**
	(ii) **müs-sen***	(ii) **sol-len***	(ii) **wol-len***	(ii) **lassen***
Future Indic.				
ich werde	müssen	sollen	wollen	lassen

*see note iv †not a modal but behaves like one.

130

Notes on modal verbs

(i) These verbs are irregular in the singular of the present tense.

(ii) They are followed by a plain infinitive, i.e. no **zu** (see p 136)

e.g. **Ich muß diese Verben lernen**

(iii) There is no umlaut in the imperfect indicative of **dürfen, können, mögen, müssen.**

(iv) After the infinitive of another verb the infinitive and not the past participle is used in the perfect and pluperfect tenses.

e.g. **Er hat es gemocht** but **Er hat es tun mögen**

Er hat es gewollt but **Er hat das Buch lesen wollen**

(v) The subjunctive forms follow the weak verb pattern (see p 128).

Some uses of modal verbs

Dürfen
Er durfte alles machen He was allowed to do anything
Es dürfte wahr sein It may be true

Können
Es kann sein It may be
Es kann vielleicht regnen It may rain
Er kann Deutsch He knows German
Ich kann nichts dafür I can't help it
Er kann es unmöglich tragen He can't possibly carry it
Ich kann es getan haben I may have done it
Ich habe es tun können I was able to do it

Mögen
Er mag kommen He may come
Das mag wohl sein That may be
Es mag wohl zehn Tage her sein It must be about ten days ago
Er mag zwei Jahre alt gewesen sein He may have been two years old
Ich möchte Deutschland besuchen I should like to visit Germany

Müssen
Ich mußte es tun I had to do it
Er muß es getan haben He must have done it
Er hat es tun müssen He has had to do it

Sollen

Was soll das? What does that mean?
Er soll reich sein He is supposed (said) to be rich
Der Kranke soll zu Bett gehen The sick man is to go to bed
Der Wagen sollte uns zum Bahnhof bringen The car was to take us
  to the station
Was sollte ich anfangen? What was I to do?
Er sollte (subjunc) **es tun** He ought to do it
Er hätte es tun sollen He ought to have done it
Er soll es getan haben He is supposed (said) to have done it

Wollen

Wollen Sie mitkommen? Do you want to come with us?
Wir wollen ins Kino gehen! Let's go to the pictures (see p 137)
Ich will eben ausgehen I am just going out
Ich wollte eben ausgehen I was just going out

Lassen

Ich ließ es dort liegen I left it lying there
Laß uns gehen! Let's go (see p 137)
Er hat mich warten lassen He made me wait
Er ließ sich ein Haus bauen He had a house built
Das läßt sich nicht leugnen That can't be denied
Er hat den Arzt kommen lassen He sent for the doctor
Er läßt Sie grüßen He sends his best wishes
Laß dich nicht stören Don't let me disturb you

COMPOUND VERBS

Inseparable prefixes

Verbs compounded with the following prefixes are inseparable.

be-	ent-	ge-	ver-
emp-	er-	miß -	zer-

Separable or inseparable prefixes

The following prefixes may be separable or inseparable:

durch-	über-	unter-	wider-
hinter-	um-	voll-	wieder-

They are usually separable if the verb can be translated literally
e.g. **übersetzen: Er setzte mich über** He ferried me across.
      Er übersetzte das Buch He translated the book.

Separable prefixes

All other prefixes are separable.

N.B. (i) The separable prefix goes to the end of the clause except when the infinitive or past participle is used and in subordinate clauses.

(ii) When the infinitive is used with **zu** the **zu** is put between the prefix and the verb. E.g. **er versuchte, auszusteigen**.

(iii) **ge-** is retained in the past participle (see p 120)

REFLEXIVE VERBS

There are two types of reflexive verbs. In one the pronoun is the direct object and so accusative; in the other it is a dative of possession.

Accusative	*Dative*
ich wasche mich	**ich wasche mir die Hände**
du wäschst dich	**du wäschst dir die Hände**
er, sie, es wäscht sich	**er, sie, es wäscht sich die Hände**
wir waschen uns	**wir waschen uns die Hände**
ihr wascht euch	**ihr wascht euch die Hände**
sie waschen sich	**sie waschen sich die Hände**
Sie waschen sich	**Sie waschen sich die Hände**

N.B. (i) The reflexive pronoun follows the subject as closely as possible.

(ii) **Er wäscht seine Hände:** The hands do not belong to the subject.

THE PASSIVE

Formation

The passive is formed by using the appropriate tense of **werden** (see pp 122—3) plus the past participle of the verb to be put in the passive.

N.B. (i) This past participle goes to the end of the clause.

(ii) When the perfect or pluperfect of **werden** is used, **worden** not **geworden** is used and follows the other past participle.

By

The English word'by'is expressed

(a) by **von** when it refers to the agent or agency, e.g. **Der Ball wurde von dem Jungen geschlagen, Der Baum wurde vom Sturm umrissen.**

(b) by **durch** to express means, e.g. **Er wurde von seiner Mutter durch ein heftiges Schütteln geweckt.**

(c) by **mit** to express the instrument, e.g. **Der Brief war mit einer Feder geschrieben worden.**

The infinitive ·

The passive infinitive is formed by using the past participle of the verb plus **werden**, e.g. **Er konnte von allen gehört werden.**

Sometimes by **sein + zu +** the infinitive, e.g. **Niemand war zu sehen.**

Avoidance of the passive

(a) by using a reflexive verb, e.g. **Die Tür öffnete sich.**
(b) by using **man** with an active verb, e.g. **Man öffnete die Tür.**

THE CONDITIONAL

Formation

Formed by using the imperfect subjunctive of **werden** (see p123) plus the infinitive of the verb.

Uses

(a) Used of an action that was to take place at some future time
e.g. **Ich wußte, daß er kommen würde.**

(b) In some conditional sentences (see p 163)
e.g. **Ich würde es machen, wenn ich Zeit hätte.**

The conditional perfect

This is usually replaced by the pluperfect subjunctive
e.g. **Ich hätte es getan** rather than **Ich würde es getan haben.**

IMPERSONAL VERBS

The following verbs are used impersonally.

(N.B. the use of the dative with most of them.)

    einfallen to occur to. e.g. **Es fällt mir ein.**

    fehlen (an + dative) to lack (something). e.g. **Es fehlt mir an Büchern.**

    freuen to be glad. e.g. **Es freut mich, daß** . . .

    gefallen to please, **mißfallen** to displease. e.g. **Es gefällt mir** (I like).

    gelingen to succeed, **mißlingen** to fail. e.g. **Es gelingt mir** (I manage, succeed).

N.B. the following phrases using verbs impersonally.

    Was fehlt dir? What's the matter with you?

    Es geht mir gut I am well

    Wie geht's dir How are you?

    Mir ist, als ob I feel as if

    Es ist mir warm (kalt) I am warm (cold)

    Es schadet nichts It doesn't matter

    Es tut mir leid I am sorry

    Es tut mir weh It hurts me

VERBS GOVERNING THE DATIVE

antworten to answer (someone)
befehlen to command
begegnen to meet
danken to thank
dienen to serve
drohen to threaten
einfallen to occur to (see above)
entgehen } to escape from
entkommen }
erlauben to allow
folgen to follow
gefallen to please (see above)
gehorchen to obey

gehören to belong to
gelingen to succeed (see above)
gleichen to resemble, look like
gratulieren to congratulate
glauben to believe (someone)
helfen to help
leid tun um to be sorry for (see above)
mißfallen to displease (see above)
passen to suit
raten to advise
trauen to trust
verzeihen to forgive

weh tun to hurt (see p 135) **zuhören** to listen to
widersprechen to contradict **zusehen** to watch
e.g. **Seine Mutter hilft ihm bei den Schulaufgaben.**
  Ich bin ihm begegnet.
N.B. This is not a complete list but contains most of the common verbs.

THE DEPENDENT INFINITIVE WITH AND WITHOUT *ZU*

Modal verbs (see p 129)

Zu is not required before the infinitive after a modal verb
e.g. **Ich kann diese Aufgaben leicht machen.**
  Er wollte in die Stadt gehen.

Lassen, bleiben, fühlen, hören, sehen

Zu is not required before an infinitive used with these verbs
e.g. **Ich ließ den Hund weglaufen**
  Er läßt sich ein Haus bauen He is having a house built.
  Er blieb da sitzen
  Ich fühlte die Katze schnurren
  Ich sah ihn kommen

Heißen, helfen, lehren, lernen

In short simple sentences or ones in which these verbs follow their
dependent infinitive **zu** is not required
e.g. **Er hieß den Kellner kommen**
  Er lehrt mich schwimmen
  Er half seiner Mutter aufräumen
  Er wird mich schwimmen lehren
  Die Mutter hat die Tochter stricken gelehrt
  Ich habe schwimmen gelernt

In longer sentences or ones in which the dependent infinitive follows
the verb, **zu** is required
e.g. **Wer hat dich geheißen, hierher zu kommen?**
  Sein Vater hat ihn gelehrt, einen Wagen zu fahren
  Er half mir, den Wagen bis zur Garage zu bringen
  Er hat endlich gelernt, seinen eigenen Namen zu schreiben

136

Other verbs and verbal expressions

After all other verbs and verbal expressions **zu** is needed

e.g. **Er bat mich zu kommen**

Es ist leicht, das zu sagen

N.B. for the position of **zu** with separable verbs see p 133.

IMPERATIVES

Du form

(a) Add -*e* to the verb stem

e.g. **laufen —laufe!**

N.B. This -*e* is often omitted, especially in direct speech

e.g. **Komm schnell! Trag die Teller in die Küche!**

(b) If the stem vowel changes from **e** to **ie** or **i** drop the -*st* ending from the **du** form present tense.

e.g. **nehmen—du nimmst —nimm!   lesen—du liest— lies!**

Ihr form

Use the **ihr** form present tense without the **ihr**

e.g. **geben—ihr gebt—gebt!**

Sie form

Invert the **Sie** form of the present tense

e.g. **geben—Sie geben—geben Sie!**

Wir form

Formed in one of three ways:

(a) Invert the **wir** form present tense

e.g. **gehen—wir gehen—gehen wir!**

(b) Using **wollen**

e.g. **wir wollen gehen!**

(c) Using **lassen**

e.g. **laß (laßt** or **lassen Sie) uns gehen!**

N.B. All imperatives should be followed by an exclamation mark.

Sein, haben and werden

	Du	Ihr	Sie
Sein	Sei!	Seid!	Seien Sie!
Haben	Habe!	Habt!	Haben Sie!
Werden	Werde!	Werdet!	Werden Sie!

Reflexives

	Du	Ihr	Sie
Accusative	Wasche dich!	Wascht euch!	Waschen Sie sich!
Dative	Wasche dir die Hände!	Wascht euch die Hände!	Waschen Sie sich die Hände!

PRESENT PARTICIPLES

Formation

Formed by adding **-d** to the infinitive
e.g. **kommen—kommend**

Use

Normally used only as adjectives and therefore take the normal adjectival endings (see pp 141—3).
e.g. **ein dauernder Erfolg**
(See also below)

ENGLISH VERBAL FORMS IN -ING

These can be translated in several ways.

(a) By a present participle used adjectively (see above)
e.g. **Die folgende Geschichte** The following story.

(b) By an infinitive used as a noun (N.B. these are always neuter)
e.g. **Ich bin des Stehens müde** I'm tired of standing.

(c) By the simple infinitive after **bleiben, finden, fühlen, hören, lassen** and **sehen**.

e.g. **Ich ließ es dort liegen** I left it lying there.

(d) The infinitive with **zu** when there is no change in the subject.

e.g. after **ohne, anstatt,** etc.

e.g. **Er kam ins Zimmer, ohne mich zu sehen** He came into the room without seeing me.

Es ist leicht, Deutsch zu lernen Learning German is easy.

(e) By a dependent clause, e.g. introduced by **indem** (by -ing), **daß, ohne daß, anstatt daß, da, nachdem, ehe,** etc.

e.g. **Er kam ins Zimmer, ohne daß ich ihn sah** He came into the room without my seeing him.

(f) By a dependent clause introduced by **wie** after verbs of seeing or hearing.

e.g. **Ich hörte, wie er die Treppe hinaufkam** I heard him coming up the stairs.

(g) By a relative clause

e.g. **Der Mann, der die Zeitung las, schlief ein** The man reading the paper fell asleep.

(h) By a main clause introduced by **und**

e.g. **Er schlief fest und wachte um 9 Uhr auf** He slept soundly, waking at 9 o'clock.

(i) The past participle of a verb of motion after **kommen**

e.g. **Er kam auf mich zugelaufen** He came running up to me.

(j) By a finite verb with **gern, lieber, am liebsten**

e.g. **Ich spiele gern Fußball** I like playing football.

(k) By a preposed adjectival clause

e.g. **Die Fußball spielenden Kinder machten viel Lärm** The children playing football made a lot of noise.

(l) Note also the continuous sense of the various tenses

Ich schreibe einen Brief I am writing a letter

Er las die Zeitung He was reading the paper

Er hat dem Fernsehen zugesehen He has been watching television

Ich hatte im Wohnzimmer gearbeitet I had been working in the lounge (living room)

TENSES AFTER *SEIT*

Note the differences between the English tenses and the German ones used after **seit.**

(a) **Seit wann lernen Sie Deutsch?** How long have you been learning German?

The Germans use the present tense because you have been and still are learning German.

(b) **Er wohnte seit zwei Jahren in Berlin, als der Krieg begann** He had been living in Berlin for two years when the war began.

The Germans use the imperfect because he had been and still was living in Berlin.

N.B. The Germans use the same tense as the English if the sentence is negative.

e.g. **Ich habe ihn seit Jahren nicht gesehen** I haven't seen him for years.

Adjectives

Agreement of adjectives

Adjectives used predicatively do not decline
e.g. **Der Mann ist gut — Die Männer sind gut.**
But if an adjective precedes its noun then the appropriate ending must be added. There are six groups of endings.

(a) *Der* group
After **der, dieser, jener, jeder, solcher, welcher** and **mancher** (sing.) the following endings are added.

	M.	F.	N.	Pl.
N.	-E	-E	-E	-EN
A.	-EN	-E	-E	-EN
G.	-EN	-EN	-EN	-EN
D.	-EN	-EN	-EN	-EN

e.g. **Der alte Mann hat die neuen Bücher.**
Die junge Frau wohnt in dem neuen Haus.

(b) *Ein* group
After **ein**

	M.	F.	N.	Pl.
N.	-ER	-E	-ES	-E
A.	-EN	-E	-ES	-E
G.	-EN	-EN	-EN	-ER
D.	-EN	-EN	-EN	-EN

e.g. **Neue Bücher liegen auf einem runden Tisch.**

(c) *Kein* group
After **kein** and the possessive adjectives (see p 145).

	M.	F.	N.	Pl.
N.	-ER	-E	-ES	-EN
A.	-EN	-E	-ES	-EN
G.	-EN	-EN	-EN	-EN
D.	-EN	-EN	-EN	-EN

e.g. **Seine junge Tochter hat keine alten Puppen.**

(d) *No defining word*

	M.	F.	N.	Pl.
N.	-ER	-E	-ES	-E
A.	-EN	-E	-ES	-E
G.	-EN	-ER	-EN	-ER
D.	-EM	-ER	-EM	-EN

e.g. **Nach vielen Tagen sonnig*en* Wetters**

(e) *After* **einige, wenige, ein paar, manche** *(plural)*, **viele** *and* **mehrere.**

	Pl.
N.	-E
A.	-E
G.	-ER
D.	-EN

e.g. **Ein paar reich*e* Leute wohnen in vielen groß*en* Häusern**

(f) *After Alle*

The demonstrative or possessive adjective after **alle** has the same ending as **alle**. Any other adjective takes -*en.*

e.g. N. **alle diese (meine) neuen Bücher**
   A. **alle diese (meine) neuen Bücher**
   G. **aller dieser (meiner) neuen Bücher**
   D. **allen diesen (meinen) neuen Büchern**

Adjectives after *nichts* etc.

After **etwas, viel, soviel, wenig, nichts** and **allerlei** the adjective is written with a capital letter* and takes the following endings.

N.	-ES
A.	-ES
G.	-EN
D.	-EM

e.g. **Ich habe nichts Neues gesehen.**

---

*ander, möglich, übrig and einzig are exceptions and retain the small letter.
e.g. etwas anderes.

Adjectives after *alles* etc.

After **alles, vieles** and **weniges** the adjective is written with a capital letter* and takes the following endings

N.	**-E**
A.	**-E**
G.	**-EN**
D.	**-EN**

e.g. **Ich wünsche dir alles Gute**

*ander, möglich, übrig** and **einzig** retain the small letter.

THE COMPARATIVE AND SUPERLATIVE

Stems

To form the comparative stem add *-er* to the adjective.
To form the superlative stem add *-(e)st* to the adjective.
N.B. Most monosyllabic adjectives add an umlaut.

e.g.	*Positive*	*Comparative*	*Superlative*
	schnell	**schneller**	**schnellst**
	warm	**wärmer**	**wärmst**

Declension

Comparative and superlative adjectives decline like normal adjectives.
(see pp 141—3).
e.g. **ein schneller Zug — der schnellste Zug**

Predicative superlative

Add *-(e)sten* to the adjective and put **am** in front.
e.g. **Der Schwarzwald ist im Winter am schönsten.** Hier ist
   der Fluß am breitesten.
Additional examples: **Koblenz ist groß, Köln ist größer, Berlin**
   ist am größten

Than and as

longer than **länger *als***
not longer than **nicht länger *als***
not so long as **nicht *so* lang *wie***
as long as **(eben) *so* lang *wie***

Irregular adjectives

Positive	Comparative	Superlative
groß	größer	größt
hoch	höher	höchst
viel[1]	mehr[2]	die meisten (pl. only)
gut	besser	best
nah	näher	nächst

[1] does not decline in the singular (except **Vielen Dank**)
[2] does not decline

False superlatives

e.g. He is most clever **Er ist höchst (äußerst) klug.**

Note the following construction
Immer besser better and better   **Immer mehr** more and more
Immer schneller quicker and quicker   .

ADJECTIVES FORMED FROM PLACE NAMES

Adjectives can be formed from names of cities etc. by adding -*er* to the place name.

N.B. (i) these adjectives have a capital letter.

(ii) they do not decline

e.g. **Der Nürnberger Dom   Die Berliner Straßen**

ADJECTIVES USED AS NOUNS

When adjectives are used as nouns they are
(i) *declined* liked ordinary adjectives (see pp 141–3).
(ii) written with a *capital letter*

(*Masculine*)

Singular	Plural	Singular	Plural
der Fremde	die Fremden	ein Fremder	Fremde
den Fremden	die Fremden	einen Fremden	Fremde
des Fremden	der Fremden	eines Fremden	Fremder
dem Fremden	den Fremden	einem Fremden	Fremden

Wohnt die alte Frau hier?   Ja, *die Alte* wohnt hier.
Kennst du den alten Mann?   Ja, ich kenne *den Alten*.
Der Mann der alten Frau ist krank.   Der Mann *der Alten* ist krank.

**Was gibt die alte Frau ihrem kranken Mann? Sie gibt
ihrem Kranken Medizin.**

The most common adjectival nouns are:

der Alte, ein Alter old man
der Beamte, ein Beamter official
der Bekannte, ein Bekannter acquaintance
der Deutsche, ein Deutscher German
der Erwachsene, ein Erwachsener adult
der Fremde, ein Fremder stranger, foreigner
der Reisende, ein Reisender traveller
der Verwandte, ein Verwandter relative

Der Reisende sprach mit dem Beamten an der Grenze.
Wir besuchten unsere Verwandten in Berlin.
Ich begegnete einem Bekannten in der Stadt.

POSSESSIVE ADJECTIVES

Stems

ich —**mein** my	**wir** —**unser** our
du —**dein** your	**ihr** —**euer** your
er —**sein** his, its	
sie —**ihr** her, its	**sie** —**ihr** their
es —**sein** its	
Sie —**Ihr** your	**Sie** —**Ihr** your

Declension

To these stems are added the following endings

	M.	F.	N.	Pl.
N	-	-E	-	-E
A.	-EN	-E	-	-E
G.	-ES	-ER	-ES	-ER
D.	-EM	-ER	-EM	-EN

N.B. (i) When **euer** has an ending it drops its second **e**
e.g. **Euer Vater** but **das Buch eures Vaters**

(ii) Similarly the **e** may also be omitted from **unser** when it has an ending.

e.g. **Unsere Bücher** or **unsre Bücher**

Pronouns

Personal pronouns

Nom.	Acc.	Dat.	Nom.	Acc.	Dat.
ich	mich	mir	wir	uns	uns
du	dich	dir	ihr	euch	euch
er	ihn	ihm ⎫			
sie	sie	ihr ⎬	sie	sie	ihnen
es	es	ihm ⎭			
Sie	Sie	Ihnen	Sie	Sie	Ihnen

N.B. (i) If the pronoun refers to a thing or things and is governed by a preposition, **da (dar)** plus the preposition is used instead of the pronoun.

e.g. **mit dem Lehrer — mit ihm**　but **mit dem Bleistift — damit
auf dem Stuhl — darauf**

(ii) 'it' can be masculine or feminine as well as neuter in German depending on the gender of the noun it replaces.

Interrogative pronouns

	Persons	Things
N.	wer	was
A.	wen	was (**wo/wor** + preposition)
G.	wessen	wessen
D.	wem	**wo/wor** + preposition.

N.B. If the pronoun refers to a thing or things and is governed by a preposition, **wo(wor)** plus the preposition is used instead of the pronoun (cf. note on personal pronouns).

e.g. **Er geht mit dem Vater spazieren —** *mit wem* **geht er spazieren?** but **Er schreibt mit dem Bleistift —** *womit* **schreibt er?**

Relative pronouns

	M.	F.	N.	Pl.
N.	der	die	das	die
A.	den	die	das	die
G.	dessen	deren	dessen	deren
D.	dem	der	dem	denen

N.B. (i) The relative pronoun agrees in number and gender with the noun to which it refers.

(ii) The case of the pronoun depends on the part it plays in the relative clause.

(iii) The relative pronoun clause immediately follows the antecedent.

(iv) The verb goes to the end of the relative clause.

(v) The relative clause is separated from the rest of the sentence by commas.

(vi) If the pronoun is governed by a preposition and refers to a thing or things, **wo(wor)** plus the preposition may be used instead of the pronoun.

e.g. **Die Frau, deren Sohn krank war, war traurig. Das Haus, wovor (or vor dem) ich stehe, ist sehr alt.**

N.B. The relative pronoun cannot be omitted in German as it is in English.

e.g. The book I am reading is interesting. **Das Buch, das ich lese, ist interessant.**

Reflexive pronouns

(Cf. reflexive verbs p 133)

	Acc.	Dat.		Acc.	Dat.
ich	mich	mir	wir	uns	uns
du	dich	dir	ihr	euch	euch
er					
sie	sich	sich	sie	sich	sich
es					
Sie	sich	sich	Sie	sich	sich

e.g. **Er machte die Tür hinter sich zu** He shut the door behind him (self).

Er hat sich das Bein gebrochen He has broken his leg.

Ein and the possessive adjectives used as pronouns

Add the following endings to the stem (see p 145)

	M.	F.	N.	Pl.
N.	-ER	-E	-ES	-E
A.	-EN	-E	-ES	-E
G.	-ES	-ER	-ES	-ER
D.	-EM	-ER	-EM	-EN

N.B. (i) The pronoun thus formed is the same gender as the noun to which it refers.

(ii) Its case depends on the part it plays in the sentence.

e.g. **Dein Bruder ist älter als mein*er*.**
     Er spricht mit ein*er* meiner Freundinnen.

N.B. also **der mein(ig)e, die mein(ig)e, das mein(ig)e, die mein(ig)en**, etc.
e.g. **Hier ist mein Buch. Wo is das dein(ig)e?**

Adverbs

Formation

Almost all adjectives can also be used as adverbs, e.g. **die schöne Frau singt schön**.

N.B. The following are common exceptions.

blindlings blindly	**teils** } partly
(un)glücklicherweise	**teilweise** }
(un)fortunately	**vorwärts** (etc.) forwards
lange for a long time	**wochenlang** (etc.) for weeks
morgens (etc.) in the morning	

Order of adverbs

If two or more adverbs or adverbial phrases occur in a sentence they must come in the following order.

1. TIME   2. MANNER   3. PLACE

e.g. **Jeden Morgen fahre ich mit dem Bus in die Stadt.**

If two adverbs of the same sort occur in a sentence the more general precedes the more specific.

e.g. **Er saß im Garten unter dem Apfelbaum.**

COMPARATIVE AND SUPERLATIVE

Regular adverbs

(i) The comparative is formed by adding *-er* to the positive form.

(ii) The superlative is formed by adding *-(e)sten* to the positive form and putting **am** in front.

(iii) Most adverbs of one syllable take an umlaut in the comparative and superlative.

e.g. *Positive*	*Comparative*	*Superlative*
kalt	**kälter**	**am kältesten**
freundlich	**freundlicher**	**am freundlichsten**

Irregular adverbs

Positive	Comparative	Superlative
bald	eher	am ehesten
	früher	am frühsten
gern	lieber	am liebsten
gut (wohl)	besser	am besten
oft (häufig)	öfter	am öftesten
	häufiger	am häufigsten
viel (sehr)	mehr	am meisten
wenig	weniger	am wenigsten
	minder	am mindesten

Prepositions

Governing the accusative

ausgenommen except
bis till, to, as far as
durch through, by
entlang along
für for, on behalf of

gegen against, towards, about
ohne without
um round, at
wider against

N.B. **Ausgenommen** and **entlang** follow their nouns.

Governing the genitive

(an)statt instead of
außerhalb outside
diesseits this side of
inmitten among
innerhalb inside
jenseits the other side of
kraft by virtue of
(ver) mittels by means of

trotz in spite of
um . . . willen for the sake of
unterhalb below
unweit not far from
während during
wegen because of
zeit during

Governing the dative

aus out of, from
außer except
bei at (Cf. Fr. **chez**)
dank thanks to
entgegen towards
gegenüber opposite

gemäß in accordance with
mit with
nach to, after, according to
seit since, for (time)
von from, of
zu to, at

N.B. (i) **Entgegen** and **gegenüber** normally follow their nouns.
(ii) When **nach** follows its noun it means according to.

Governing the accusative or dative

an on, to, at
auf on to, on
hinter behind
in in, into
neben near, next to

über over, across, about
unter under, among
vor in front of, ago
zwischen between

N.B. (i) They govern the accusative if they show motion to a place.
e.g. **Er steckte das Geld in die Tasche.**

(ii) They govern the dative if they show

(a) rest, e.g. **Er hatte das Geld in der Tasche.**
(b) motion at a place, e.g. **Er ging im Zimmer auf und ab.**

Some common constructions with prepositions

(i) *An* + *accusative*

Er kommt an die Reihe	it is his turn
Gewohnt an	accustomed to
Denken an	to think of
Sich erinnern an	to remember
Sich gewöhnen an	to get used to

(ii) *An* + *dative*

Er ist an der Reihe **Die Reihe ist an ihm** }	it's his turn
Am Morgen (usw)	in the morning (etc.)
Am nächsten Tag (usw)	on the next day (etc.)
Der Mangel an	the lack of
Der Vorrat an	the supply of
An deiner Stelle	in your place
Nahe an	near
Schuld an	guilty of
Erkennen an	to recognise by
Leiden an	to suffer from
Sich freuen an	to be glad about
Fehlen an	to be lacking in
Teilnehmen an	to take part in
Vorbeigehen (usw) an	to walk (etc.) past

(iii) *Auf* + *accusative*

Auf das Land gehen	to go into the country
Er kam auf mich zu	he came up to me
Er kam auf zwei Tage	he came for two days
Auf diese Weise	in this way
Auf jeden Fall	in any case
Auf deutsch (usw)	in German (etc.)
Die Antwort auf	the answer to
Stolz auf	proud of
Böse auf	angry with
Achten auf Aufpassen auf }	to pay attention to
Antworten auf	to answer
Sich freuen auf	to look forward to
Hoffen auf	to hope for
Warten auf	to wait for
Sich verlassen auf	to rely on
Weisen auf Zeigen auf }	to point at
Sich auf den Weg machen	to set out

(iv) *Auf* + *dative*

Auf dem Bahnhof	at the station
Auf der Straße	in the street
Auf dem Land sein	to be in the country
Auf dem Weg	on the way
Bestehen auf	to insist on

(v) *Aus*

Er kommt/stammt aus Berlin	he comes from Berlin
Aus Holz (usw)	made of wood (etc.)
Bestehen aus	to consist of

(vi) *Ausgenommen*

Alle sind artig, ihn ausge- nommen	all are well-behaved except him

(vii) **Außer**

Außer dir sehe ich niemand	I see nobody except you
Er ist außer Atem	he is out of breath
Er ist außer sich (vor)	he is beside himself (with)

(viii) **Außerhalb**

Das Haus lag außerhalb der Stadt.	the house lay outside the town

(ix) **Bei**

Er wohnt bei seinen Eltern	he lives with his parents
Bei schlechtem Wetter	in bad weather
Bei seiner Ankunft (Rückkehr)	on his arrival (return)
Bei dieser Gelegenheit	at this opportunity
Er hat kein Geld bei sich	he has no money on him
Bei Tagesanbruch	at dawn
Bei Sonnenuntergang	at sunset
Anwesend bei	present at
Sich beklagen bei	to complain to
Sich entschuldigen bei	to apologise to
Helfen bei	to help with

(x) **Bis**

Er bleibt bis Ostern	he is staying till Easter.
Bis nächsten Sonntag ist er zurück	he'll be back by next Sunday
Neun bis zehn (9–10) Jahre	nine to ten years
Er ging bis zum Rand der Klippe	he went to the edge of the cliff
Alle arbeiteten bis auf ihn	all were working except him

(xi) **Dank**

Dank deiner Bemühung	thanks to your efforts

(xii) **Diesseits**

Diesseits des Meeres	this side of the sea

(xiii) **Durch**

Er geht durch die Stadt	he walks through the town
Er wurde durch den Lärm geweckt	he was awakened by the noise

(xiv) *Entgegen*

Er kam mir entgegen	he came towards me

(xv) *Entlang*

Er ging die Straße entlang	he walked along the street

(xvi) *Für*

Er tat es für mich	he did it for me
Jahr für Jahr	year after year
Danken für	to thank for
Sich interessieren für	to be interested in
Schwärmen für	to be very keen on
Sorgen für	to look after
Gelten für	to be considered
Er gilt für einen Narren	he is considered a fool
Halten für	to consider
Ich halte es für überflüssig	I consider it unnecessary

(xvii) *Gegen*

Wir flogen gegen den Wind	we flew against the wind
Gegen 4 Uhr	about four o'clock
Gegen Ende des Jahres	towards the end of the year
Ich bin nichts gegen ihn	I'm nothing compared with him
Freundlich gegen	friendly towards
Sich wehren gegen	to oppose
Etwas/nichts dagegen haben	to have something/nothing against it

(xviii) *Gegenüber*

Er wohnt dem Kino gegenüber	he lives opposite the cinema

(xix) *Gemäß*

Seiner Pflicht gemäß	according to his duty

(xx) *Hinter* + *accusative*

Er ging hinter das Haus	he went behind the house

(xxi) *Hinter* + *dative*

Er versteckte sich hinter dem Schrank	he was hiding behind the cupboard

(xxii) *In* + *accusative*

Ins Ausland reisen	to go abroad
Ins Freie gehen	to go into the open air
Ins Theater (usw) gehen	to go to the theatre etc.
In Ordnung bringen	to tidy
Ich schnitt mich in die Hand	I cut my hand
Eingewickelt in	wrapped in
Verliebt in	in love with
Einfallen in	to attack
Einsteigen in	to get on (trains etc.)
Eintreten in	to enter
Geraten in	to get into (difficulties etc.)

(xxiii) *In* + *dative*

In der Nähe von	near
Im Freien sein	to be in the open air
In der Nacht	at night
In dem Augenblick	at that moment
Einmal im Jahre	once a year
Im Gegenteil	on the contrary
Im allgemeinen	in general
Im Radio/Fernsehen	on the wireless/television
In einer Entfernung von	at a distance of
In Gegensatz zu	in contrast to
Ankommen in	to arrive at
Bestehen in	to consist in

(xxiv) *Inmitten*

Inmitten der Bäume	among the trees

(xxv) *Innerhalb*

Innerhalb der Stadt	inside the town
Innerhalb eines Jahres	within a year

(xxvi) *Jenseits*

Jenseits des Meeres	on the other side of the sea

(xxvii) *Kraft*

Kraft seines Ranges	by virtue of his rank

156

(xxviii) *Mit*

Er kam mit mir	he came with me
Mit Tinte (Bleistift) geschrieben	written in ink (pencil)
Mit Absicht	intentionally
Mit dem Auto (usw)	by car (etc.)
Mit leiser (lauter) Stimme	in a quiet (loud) voice
Fertig mit	finished with
Sich beschäftigen mit	to be busy with
Mit dem Kopf nicken	to nod one's head
Rechnen mit	to count on
Mit dem Schwanz wedeln	to wag one's tail
Sprechen mit	to talk to
Umgehen mit	to associate with

(xxix) *(Ver) mittels*

Mittels seiner Hilfe	with his aid

(xxx) *Nach*

Er fuhr nach Berlin	he went to Berlin
Er ging nach Hause	he went home
Nach einer Stunde	after an hour
Nach meiner Meinung } Meiner Meinung nach }	in my opinion
Der Reihe nach	in turn
Allem Anschein nach	to all appearances
In der Richtung nach	in the direction of
Sich erkundigen nach } Fragen nach }	to enquire about
Schicken nach	to send for
Schmecken nach	to taste of
Urteilen nach	to judge from
Riechen nach	to smell of
Gierig nach	eager for

(xxxi) *Neben* + *accusative*

Er stellte sich neben das Fenster	he stood near the window

(xxxii) **Neben** + *dative*
Er stand neben dem Fenster   he was standing by the window

(xxxiii) **Ohne**
Ohne seine Frau fuhr er nach   he went to America without his
  Amerika   wife

(xxxiv) **Seit**
Seit dem Krieg   since the war
Seit zwei Jahren lerne ich   I have been learning German for
  Deutsch*   two years
Ich wartete seit langem*   I had been waiting for a long time

(xxxv) **(An) statt**
Er tat es statt meiner   he did it instead of me
Statt des Weins trank er   he drank beer instead of wine
  Bier

(xxxvi) **Trotz**
Trotz des Wetters   despite the weather
(N.B. **Trotzdem:** nevertheless)

(xxxvii) **Über** + *accusative*
Er ging über die Brücke   he went over the bridge
Er fuhr über Berlin   he went via Berlin
Ein Bericht über   a report on
Froh über   glad about
Traurig über   sad about
Enttäuscht über   disappointed in
Erstaunt über   surprised at
Zornig über   angry at
Sich beklagen über   to complain about
Sich freuen über   to be glad about
Klagen über   to complain of
Lachen über   to laugh at
Sich wundern über   to be surprised at
Schreiben über   to write about

*See p 140.

(xxxviii) *Über* + *dative*

Die Möwen kreisten über   the seagulls circled over the ship
  dem Schiff

(xxxix) *Um*

Um die Stadt   round the town
Um 4 Uhr   at 4 o'clock
Um so besser   all the better
Um so mehr   all the more
Bitten um   to ask for
Bringen um   to rob of
Sich handeln um   be a question of
Sich kümmern um   to worry about

(xl) *Um . . . willen*

Um Gottes willen   for heaven's sake

(xli) *Unter* + *accusative*

Er ging unter die Brücke   he walked under the bridge

(xlii) *Unter* + *dative*

Unter den Kindern   among the children
Unter anderm   among other things
Unter dieser Bedingung   on this condition
Unter diesen Umständen   in these circumstances
Unter der Regierung von   in the reign of
Unter uns   amongst ourselves

(xliii) *Unterhalb*

Unterhalb der Brücke wird   the river widens below the bridge
  der Fluß breiter

(xliv) *Unweit*

Unweit des Dorfes lag der   the farm lay not far from the
  Bauernhof   village

(xlv) *Von*

Von Zeit zu Zeit   from time to time
Von nun an   from now on
Abhängig von   dependent on
Nördlich (usw) von   to the north (etc.) of
Von Ansehen kennen   to know by sight

Erzählen von $\rbrace$ Sagen von	to tell of
Abhalten von	to keep, prevent from
Abhängen von	to depend on
Sprechen von	to talk of
Weichen von	to budge from

(xlvi) **Vor** + *accusative*

Er stellte sich vor das Fenster	he went and stood in front of the window

(xlvii) **Vor** + *dative*

Vor einem Jahr	a year ago
Vor langer Zeit	a long time ago
Vor allen Dingen $\rbrace$ Vor allem	above all
Blaß vor	pale with
Sicher vor	safe from
Draußen vor	outside
Angst haben vor $\rbrace$ Sich fürchten vor	to be afraid of
Lachen vor Freude	to laugh with joy
Schützen vor	to protect against
Warnen vor	to warn against
Weichen vor	to give way to
Weinen vor	to cry for
Zittern vor Angst (usw)	to tremble with fear (etc.)

(xlviii) **Während**

Während der Sommerferien	during the summer holidays

(xlix) **Wegen**

Wegen des Wetters	because of the weather
Berühmt wegen	famous for
Loben wegen	to praise for
Schelten wegen	to scold for
Sich schämen wegen	to be ashamed because of
Tadeln wegen	to blame for
N.B. Meinetwegen, deinetwegen (usw)	for my sake, your sake, etc.

(l) *Wider*

Normally indicates mental or moral opposition

Er tat es wider meinen Willen he did it against my wish

Wider Willen   reluctantly

N.B. Verbs compounded with **wider** govern the dative (see p 135)

(li) *Zeit*

Zeit meines Lebens	during my life

(lii) *Zu*

Er ging zum Bahnhof	he went to the station
Er ging zur Schule	he went to school
Er ging zu Bett	he went to bed
Zu Hause	at home
Zu Fuß	on foot
Zu Ostern, Pfingsten, Weih-nachten	at Easter, Whitsun, Christmas
Zu Mittag (Abend) essen	to have lunch (dinner)
Eine Briefmarke zu 30 Pf.	a 30 Pf. stamp
Zu beiden Seiten	on both sides
Zur Not	if need be
Zum Glück	fortunately
Zum Beispiel	for example
Das Gasthaus zum Löwen	the 'Lion' inn
Zu meinem Erstaunen	to my surprise
Bringen zu	to make, provoke
Gehören zu	to belong to (i.e. to be part of)
Verurteilen zu	to condemn to
Wählen zu	to elect
Werden zu	to become

(lii) *Zwischen* + *accusative*

Er setzte sich zwischen die beiden Jungen	he sat down between the two boys

(liv) *Zwischen* + *dative*

Er saß zwischen den beiden Jungen	he was sitting between the two boys

Miscellaneous

Indirect speech and question

(i)   In indirect speech and question the verb is in the subjunctive (see p 128).

(ii) In an indirect question the verb is sent to the end of the clause.

(iii) The Germans prefer to omit the conjunction 'that' (**daß**) in indirect speech.

(iv) *Scheme of tenses*

In indirect speech the German should retain the same tense as the original direct speech, provided the subjunctive and indicative forms of the verb are different. If they are identical, the verb in the indirect speech is put back one tense in the past (e.g. present to imperfect).

e.g. *Direct Speech*   *Indirect Speech*

(a) **Er ist traurig**   **Er sagte, er sei traurig**
     The forms are different so the present subjunctive is used in the indirect speech.

     Ich habe ein Buch   **Er sagte, ich hätte** (not **habe**)
                                  ein Buch
     The form of the present subjunctive would be identical to the present indicative, so the imperfect subjunctive is used.

(b) **Er hat die Aufgabe**   **Er sagte, er habe die Aufgabe**
     gemacht   **gemacht**
     Perfect subjunctive because the forms are different.

     Sie haben die Aufgabe   **Er sagte, sie hätten** (not **haben**)
     gemacht   **die Aufgabe gemacht**
     Pluperfect, not perfect, because the forms are identical.

This may be summarised as follows (the tense in brackets is the one to be used if the indicative and subjunctive forms are identical):

Direct Speech	Indirect Speech
(a) Present Indicative	Present Subjunctive (Imperfect Subjunctive)
(b) Imperfect Indicative Perfect Indicative Pluperfect Indicative	Perfect Subjunctive (Pluperfect Subjunctive)
(c) Future Indicative Conditional	Future Subjunctive (Conditional)

N.B. In an Indirect Question the word for 'if' is **ob**.´

Conditional sentences

(i) *Types*

(a) **Wenn ich müde bin, so gehe ich zu Bett.** If I am tired I go to bed.

(b) **Wenn ich müde bin, so werde ich zu Bett gehen.** If I am tired I shall go to bed.

(c) **Wenn ich müde wäre,** { **so würde ich zu Bett gehen.** **so ginge ich zu Bett.**

   If I were tired I would go to bed.

(d) **Wenn ich müde gewesen wäre, so wäre ich zu Bett gegangen.** If I had been tired I would have gone to bed.´

N.B. Word order!

In (a) and (b) the verbs are in the indicative.

In (c) and (d) the verbs are in the subjunctive.

In type (c) the conditional is normally used in the **so** clause and must be used if the subjunctive and indicative forms are identical.

Wenn clause	*So clause*
(a) Present Indicative	Present Indicative
(b) Present Indicative	Future Indicative
(c) Imperfect Subjunctive	{ Conditional Imperfect Subjunctive
(d) Pluperfect Subjunctive	Pluperfect Subjunctive

163

(ii) *Omission of* **so** *and* **wenn**

(a) **Wenn** may be omitted if **so** is used.

e.g. **Bin ich müde, so gehe ich zu Bett.**

N.B. New word order — verb first.

(b) **So** may be omitted if **wenn** is used.

e.g. **Wenn ich müde bin, gehe ich zu Bett.**

(c) If the **so** clause precedes the **wenn** clause, **so** is omitted and normal word order applies.

e.g. **Ich gehe zu Bett, wenn ich müde bin.**

Word order

(i) *Verbs*

(a) The main verb must be the second idea in the sentence unless it is the imperative or interrogative form.

e.g. **Sie stehen um sieben Uhr auf.**
    Wenn es sieben Uhr ist, stehen Sie auf.
    Stehen Sie um sieben Uhr auf!
    Stehen Sie um sieben Uhr auf?

(b) Infinitives and past participles go to the end of the clause.

(c) Verbs go to the end of subordinate clauses (see section v).

(d) If there are two infinitives in a sentence and the finite verb is sent to the end then it will precede these infinitives.

e.g. **Ich weiß, daß er wird kommen können.**
    Er sagte, daß er das Buch nicht habe finden können.

(ii) *Nicht*

Nicht goes as near the end of the sentence as possible unless it is making a particular word negative when it precedes that word.

e.g. **Ich kann ihn nicht sehen** I cannot see him.
    Ich kann ihn nicht heute sehen I cannot see him today.

(iii) *Adverbs* (see p 149)

    1. Time   2. Manner   3. Place

e.g. **Jeden Tag fährt er mit dem Bus in die Schule.**

If two or more adverbs of the same type occur in a sentence the more general precedes the more specific.

e.g. **Er kommt jeden Tag um 4 Uhr nach Hause.**

164

(iv) *Objects*

(a) If both the direct and indirect objects are nouns the indirect precedes the direct.

e.g. **Er gibt dem Mann das Buch.**

(b) If they are both pronouns the direct precedes the indirect.

e.g. **Er gibt es ihm.**

(c) If one is a noun and the other a pronoun the pronoun always comes first.

e.g. **Er gibt ihm das Buch.   Er gibt es dem Mann.**

(v) *Conjunctions*

(a) *Coordinating*, i.e. do not affect word order.

aber but	**oder** or
allein but (literary)	**sondern** but
denn for	**und** and

e.g. **Ich will zu Bett gehen, denn ich bin müde.**

N.B. **Sondern** and not **aber** must be used when

    (i) The preceding clause is negative.

    (ii) Both clauses have the same subject.

    (iii) The second clause directly contradicts the first, e.g. **Sie sind nicht reich, aber glücklich** but **Sie sind nicht reich, sondern arm.**

(b) *Adverbial*, i.e. require inversion of verb and subject.

also		**dennoch**	yet, nevertheless
so	therefore,	**(je)doch**	
daher	and so	**deswegen**	that is why, therefore.
darum		**deshalb**	
auch	also, too	**indessen**	meanwhile
auch . . . nicht	nor, neither	**inzwischen**	
außerdem	besides,	**unterdessen**	
übrigens	moreover	**kaum**	hardly, scarcely
da	then, so	**sonst**	otherwise, else
		trotzdem	in spite of that
		und zwar	in fact

e.g. **Es war kalt, deswegen sind wir zu Hause geblieben. Wir müssen eilen, sonst verpassen wir den Zug.**

165

(c) *Subordinating*, i.e. send the verb to the end of the clause.
Almost all conjunctions other than those listed in (a) and (b) are
subordinating.

e.g. **Weil es kalt war, trug er ein Paar Handschuhe. Ich wußte,
daß er zu Hause war.**

Numerals

(i) *Cardinal numbers*

1	**eins**	21	**einundzwanzig**
2	**zwei**	22.	**zweiundzwanzing**, etc.
3	**drei**	30	**dreißig**
4	**vier**	31	**einunddreißig**, etc.
5	**fünf**	40	**vierzig**
6	**sechs**	50	**fünfzig**
7	**sieben**	60	**sechzig**
8	**acht**	70	**siebzig**
9	**neun**	80	**achtzig**
10	**zehn**	90	**neunzig**
11	**elf**	100	**hundert**
12	**zwölf**	101	**hunderteins**, etc.
13	**dreizehn**	110	**hundertzehn**, etc.
14	**vierzehn**	200	**zweihundert**, etc.
15	**fünfzehn**	1,000	**tausend**
16	**sechzehn**	1,001	**tausendeins**, etc.
17	**siebzehn**	2,200	**zweitausend zweihundert**
18	**achtzehn**	1,000,000	**eine Million**
19	**neunzehn**		
20	**zwanzig**		

(ii) *Ordinal numbers*

1—19: add *-te* to the cardinal number, e.g. **der zweite,** except for
eins — **der erste   dréi** — **der dritte   acht** — **der achte**

20 and over add *-ste* to the cardinal numbers
e.g. **der dreiundreißigste**

101 and over start again, e.g. **der hundertzweite, der hundert-
zwanzigste.**

(iii) *Fractions*, etc.

1/3 **ein Drittel**   1/4 **ein Viertel** etc. (all neuter), but 1/2 **die Hälfte**
1/2 **halb**

N.B.   half an apple **ein halber Apfel**
      half the apple **die Hälfte des Apfels**
      $1\frac{1}{2}$ **anderthalb** or **eineinhalb**
      $2\frac{1}{2}$ **zweieinhalb**, etc.
      -times *-mal* e.g. **einmal, zweimal**, etc.
      -ly, **erstens, zweitens**, etc.
      -fold *-fach*, e.g. **einfach, zweifach**, etc.
      kinds of *-erlei*, e.g. **einerlei, zweierlei**, etc. N.B. **allerlei** all
        kinds of

Time

Wie spät ist es? } What is the time?
Wieviel Uhr ist es? }

1.00   **es ist eins**
       es ist ein Uhr
1.05   **es ist fünf (Minuten) nach eins**
       es ist ein Uhr fünf
1.15   **es ist Viertel zwei***
       es ist Viertel nach eins
       es ist ein Uhr fünfzehn
1.30   **es ist halb zwei***
       es ist ein Uhr dreißig
1.40   **es ist zwanzig (Minuten) vor zwei**
       es ist ein Uhr vierzig
1.45   **es ist dreiviertel zwei***
       es ist Viertel vor zwei
       es ist ein Uhr fünfundvierzig
1.59   **es ist eine Minute vor zwei**
       es ist ein Uhr neunundfünfzig

to **vor**   past **nach**
12 noon **Mittag; zwölf Uhr**
12 midnight **Mitternacht; vierundzwanzig Uhr**

*N.B. The differences between the English — quarter past *one* — and the
German — quarter *two*, etc.

a.m. **morgens, vormittags.**
p.m. **nachmittags** (up to *c*. 6 p.m.)
    abends (up to *c*. 10 p.m.)
    nachts (after *c*. 10 p.m., including the early hours of the morning
    which can also be **morgens**)
N.B. at 1 o'clock **um ein Uhr**
    about 1 o'clock **gegen ein Uhr, etwa um ein Uhr**
    am Tag by day
    am Morgen
    am Vormittag } in the morning
    am Nachmittag in the afternoon
    am Abend in the evening
    BUT **in der Nacht** at night.

Dates

Days (all masc.)	*Months* (all masc.)
Monday **Montag**	January **Januar**
Tuesday **Dienstag**	February **Februar**
Wednesday **Mittwoch**	March **März**
Thursday **Donnerstag**	April **April**
Friday **Freitag**	May **Mai**
Saturday **Samstag**	June **Juni**
Sonnabend	July **Juli**
Sunday **Sonntag**	August **August**
	September **September**
	October **Oktober**
	November **November**
	December **Dezember**

Der wievielte ist es heute?
Den wievielten haben wir heute? } What is the date today?
Welches Datum haben wir heute?
Dates are formed, as in English, by using ordinal numbers (see p 166)

N.B. these numbers are adjectives and must be declined
e.g. **Heute ist der erste Januar (der 1. Januar)**

N.B. On Monday *Am* **Montag**
    On 2nd July *Am* **zweiten (2.)** *Juli*
    In July *Im* **Juli**
    In 1939 *Im* **Jahre 1939** or **1939** (never **in 1939**)

Weak masculine nouns

(a) *Adding* **-n**
e.g. **der Junge**

	Singular	*Plural*
N.	der Junge	die Jungen
A.	den Jungen	die Jungen
G.	des Jungen	der Jungen
D.	dem Jungen	den Jungen

Some common nouns in this group:

der Affe monkey	**der Kunde** customer
der Bauer farmer	**der Löwe** lion
der Bote messenger	**der Matrose** sailor
der Erbe heir	**der Neffe** nephew
der Franzose Frenchman	**der Riese** giant
der Geselle companion	**der Sklave** slave
der Knabe boy	

N.B. **Der Herr** + **-n** in the singular, + **-en** in the plural.

(b) *Adding* **-en**
e.g. **der Mensch**

	Singular	*Plural*
N.	der Mensch	die Menschen
A.	den Menschen	die Menschen
G.	des Menschen	der Menschen
D.	dem Menschen	den Menschen

Some common nouns in this group:

der Bär bear	**der Ochs** ox
der Elefant elephant	**der Prinz** prince
der Fürst prince	**der Polizist** policeman
der Held hero	**der Soldat** soldier
der Kamerad comrade	**der Student** student

(c) *Adding -n and -ns*
e.g. **der Name.**

	Singular	Plural
N.	der Name	die Namen
A.	den Namen	die Namen
G.	des Namens	der Namen
D.	dem Namen	den Namen

Some common nouns in this group:

der Friede peace   **der Haufe(n)** heap

der Gedanke thought   **der Wille** will

der Glaube belief

(d) *Das Herz*

	Singular	Plural
N.	das Herz	die Herzen
A.	das Herz	die Herzen
G.	des Herzens	der Herzen
D.	dem Herzen	den Herzen

Nouns in apposition

A noun should be in the same case as the noun or pronoun with which it stands in apposition.

e.g. **Mein Freund, der Lehrer, wohnt hier**
Kennen Sie meinen Freund, den Lehrer?
Das ist das Haus meines Freundes, des Lehrers
Ich sprach mit meinem Freund, dem Lehrer
Sie kamen am Montag, dem 20. Juli
Ein Dutzend Bücher
Mit einem Dutzend Büchern
Eine Tasse heißer Kaffee (or **heißen Kaffees**)

Note the following cases of apposition:

Die Stadt Berlin the city of Berlin
Luther ging auf die Universität Erfurt Luther went to the University of Erfurt
Eine Besichtigung der Festung Ehrenbreitstein a visit to the fortress of Ehrenbreitstein
Im Monat Mai in the month of May